CHURCHE

CHURCHES THAT OBEY

Taking the Great Commission Seriously

Edited by

Roger Forster

and

John Richard

Published on behalf of

by

First published 1995 by OM Publishing
on behalf of AD2000 and Beyond,
204 Sutton Place, Dewitt, NY 13214, U.S.A.

01 00 99 98 97 96 95   7 6 5 4 3 2 1

OM Publishing is an imprint of Send the Light Ltd.,
P.O. Box 300, Carlisle, Cumbria CA3 0QS, U.K.

British Library Cataloguing in Publication Data

Churches That Obey:Taking the Great
Commission Seriously
I. Forster, Roger II. Richard, John
269.2

ISBN 1–85078–196–6

Typeset by Photoprint, Torquay, Devon
and printed in the U.K. by Cox and Wyman Ltd., Reading

Contents

Acknowledgements and Regrets

Under God, this book has been produced by the Pastors Global Network of the AD2000 & Beyond Movement through the kind assistance of Pieter Kwant, Director of Publishing Services, and Jeremy Mudditt, Publishing Manager, at Send the Light Ltd, Doug Smith and his fellow-workers at Ichthus Christian Fellowship, all of the UK, and through the financial contributions of some churches in USA. We wish to place on record, too, our sincere gratitude to Luis Bush, International Director, AD2000 & Beyond Movement, who had first sown in our minds the seed thought to produce a book such as this, and to George Verwer, International Director of Operation Mobilisation, who encouraged us to pursue this project. More importantly, we express our deep appreciation to the pastors and leaders who, in the midst of their busy schedule, created time to provide us these articles.

Our regret is that this book does not carry accounts of what God is doing through local churches representing Europe, Latin America and the Caribbean. We had contacted some churches in those regions and in Korea, Thailand, Myanmar, etc. Sadly their submissions could not reach us by the time the manuscript had to go to the press. We are keenly conscious that the inclusion of models of such effective churches would have enhanced the worth of this book in no small measure.

Roger Forster, Chairman   John Richard, Co-ordinator
The Pastors Global Network

Introduction

D. JOHN RICHARD

'While the world has been *multiplying*, we have been *making additions* to the Church. Thus there is no hope of ever catching up.' So said a concerned church leader. This concern is factual. The Lord, however, expects us to do whatever we can while we have opportunity.

This is part of the rationale for the emergence of the AD2000 and Beyond Movement, whose Vision Statement reads: A CHURCH FOR EVERY PEOPLE AND THE GOSPEL FOR EVERY PERSON BY AD2000. In order to convert this dream into reality, the AD2000 Movement has floated a number of basic networks, one of which is the Pastors Global Network (formerly known as the Mobilization of the Local Church Track). It was felt, however, that the Movement should accord a distinct identity to Pastors and that this identity should not be hidden in the larger nomenclature of Mobilizing the Local Church.

This change, however, is not to deny the cardinal truth that the local church is foundational to the AD2000 and Beyond Movement. The local church is both the instrument and the purpose of evangelism. Therefore it must be awakened for the fulfilment of its biblical calling. This conviction and primacy of the local church arises from its theological and strategic role that it has in God's programme for the world as revealed in the Scriptures. The task of the local church is evangelism; the goal of evangelism is the local church.

To separate the pastor from the local church, however, is like trying to separate the sunlight from the sun. As is the pastor so are the people. Only he who is on fire for God can set his people on fire. And a pastor on fire for God can also inspire and enthuse other pastors. There is value in bringing pastors together if local churches are to be spiritually awakened so that these in turn can engage in world evangelization.

Networking pastors from 200 countries belonging to the non-Roman Catholic segment of the world-wide Church – the Pastors Global Network – is committed to carrying out the five-fold purpose given below:

1. To MOBILIZE Pastors so that their local churches/ assemblies will engage in the work of evangelization, missions and church planting.
2. To TRAIN our laity in the local church for the work of evangelization.
3. To ENCOURAGE Pastors and leaders to prevail on the members of their local churches to testify publicly to the Lordship of Christ through widely varied forms of witness including Praise Marches.
4. To ENABLE the Pastor to have a greater understanding of the grandeur and dignity of the ministry entrusted to him.
5. To EQUIP the Pastor with skills and tools that will enhance the effectiveness of his ministry.

We enlarge on this five-fold purpose below:

1. MOBILIZING PASTORS

The concept of unreached peoples, and the responsibility placed on local churches to establish a mission-minded church planting movement for themselves, is beginning to capture the minds of pastors. The need for 'adopting' unreached peoples is also being impressed on them. We have yet to communicate to pastors world-wide the criteria for adopting a people group.

If a people group fails to meet one of the following five requirements, then it qualifies to be adopted:

a. When the people group has not HEARD. (The gospel has not been proclaimed to them in an understandable way or form).

b. When the people group has not RESPONDED. (They do not believe that Jesus Christ is the only way to salvation and that the Bible is God's word – the truth – and live accordingly.

c. When the people group does not have a CHURCH. (Believers are not gathering together regularly for worship, teaching and outreach. A church movement has not yet started.)

d. When the people group does not have the word of God TRANSLATED into their mother tongue (written, audio or visual translations of God's word that are culturally acceptable have not been completed.)

e. When the people group does not have the word of God readily AVAILABLE. (There are practical and/or legal restrictions to distribution. A large percentage of the people is illiterate.)

Pastors need to be acquainted with the undermentioned ways and means whereby a local church can contribute toward the fulfilment of the AD2000 Vision:

a. It can set its own faith goals for the year 2000. For instance:
   i. It can pray and work towards increasing its membership.
   ii. It can work towards planting daughter churches in the neighbourhood or elsewhere.

b. It can encourage other local churches also to set faith goals for the year 2000.

c. It can initiate the convening of a small consultation for churches in the area to consider how they can individually and corporately advance the vision of the Movement.

d. It can identify women, prospective missionaries, researchers, pace-setters and warriors in the arena of prayer, and others with special aptitudes for the advance of God's kingdom.

e. It can mobilize its members to pray regularly for the '10/40 Window countries'.

f. It can adopt one or two of the 1,000 least evangelized cities as its target for intensified, warfare prayer.

g. It can gather and disseminate information about one of the 61 countries of the 10/40 Window and adopt that country for sustained prayer coverage.

h. It can join with other churches in annual Praise Marches for Jesus culminating in Concerts of Prayer in towns and cities.

i. It can encourage its members to think in terms of serving as tentmakers among unreached people groups as openings occur.

j. It can establish an AD2000 Task Force of individuals who are committed to pray and work for world evangelization.

2. TRAINING OUR LAITY

'A pastor from India writes

'Our people need to believe and practise Ephesians 4:11-16. We also need to explain to them that in order to be involved in the spreading of the gospel one does not have to be a full-time missionary or evangelist. We all have to be evangelists wherever we are . . . since we are not able to bring people to our churches to give them the gospel, we now need to take the gospel to the market place, to our offices, schools, colleges, neighbourhoods, shops, etc. And the best missionaries will be those in our churches who live and work in these places every day. We need to teach them creative means of sharing the gospel and provide all the training and resources needed to do it.'

We have always known that our laity are our 'frozen asset' which needs to be 'defrosted'. We have known too that if the world is ever to be evangelized, it can be done only by ordinary believers who scatter the word of God.

3. ENCOURAGING WITNESS

Here we specifically address ourselves to the growing movement of Praise Marches around the world. This movement is bringing together Christians of all denominations, races, ages and affiliations – a grassroots expression of living Christianity spreading world-wide and a powerful symbol of the church on the move. Its chief purpose is to proclaim Jesus publicly and forcibly, marked by a demonstration of unity, celebration and worship. Indeed, it is a manner of prophetic symbolism, the releasing of the spirit of the kingdom by action. The Pastors Network is unashamedly an ardent advocate of Praise Marches and it is encouraging pastors everywhere to get their people to take part in them.

4. THE DIGNITY OF THE PASTORAL MINISTRY

We believe that there are many countries where pastors have a low self-image. In the economically poor countries, this is even more so. These pastors need to be challenged with the grandeur and dignity of the ministry entrusted to them. They need to be taught that it is God the Father who has given them their ministry; God the Son who has commissioned them; and God the Holy Spirit who has appointed them to their ministry.

5. EQUIPPING THE PASTOR

There are churches even today which are spiritually starved because of a lack of Bible teaching. Countries which have seen phenomenal church growth are suffering from lack of trained pastors. This has given way to the rise of false teaching and has disturbed the infant faith of new converts. Furthermore, in the future there could be times of persecution when the pastors are removed from their people. Therefore the people need to learn to dig into the Scriptures for themselves.

There are also pastors who themselves need to be taught how to undertake effective expository preaching. There are already on-going efforts in this area. Our Network aims to team up with agencies who can help. We endeavour also to provide commentaries and other study aids which can enhance the effectiveness of the ministry of pastors.

F. B. Meyer, that great English Baptist preacher once said: 'The church which is not a *missionary* church will be a *missing* church when Jesus comes.' The Pastors Network commits itself to partnering other Networks in the AD2000 Movement, and also other denominations and agencies in seeing that the local churches of the world do not become missing bodies when Jesus comes.

CHAPTER 1

Witnessing to Christ

ROGER T. FORSTER

Ichthus Christian Fellowship, London

The last words of our Lord Jesus Christ to his followers
before he went back to the Father were 'You shall be my
witnesses' (Ac. 1:8). This is a promise and not a threat
from the Lord of the Church. At the same time he said
concerning this witness that it would be both — and not
simply first — 'in Jerusalem, and in all Judea, and Samaria,
and even to the remotest part of the earth' (Ac. 1:8). The
sphere of operation for our witnessing to him embraces
the world, and is not to be confined only to home
evangelization, or a particular responsibility and concern
for our own country. In the same spirit John Wesley, the
great British church leader and evangelist of the eight-
eenth century said, 'The world is my parish.'＊

Jesus precedes the call to witness with these words,
'You will receive power when the Holy Spirit comes upon
you.' This gives the time and provision that God has
appointed for this comprehensive, all-embracing, total
and primary occupation of his body; namely carrying the
good news to the world.

In the light of our Lord's promise and commission
quoted above we need:

1. FAITH

A good pastor can never be content simply to carry the burdens and solve the interminable problems of his flock, but must see that his calling is to guide the people into the great calling of the church itself, if he is to fulfil his mandate and the church fulfil hers.

Jesus' assertion that we are to be witnesses is a promise, and not just a command – therefore it must be received by faith; it is consequently the prime duty of those of us who are pastors to increase, develop and teach faith among God's people. His people are to be believers not professors. Profession, or indeed confession as Christians will arise, but only as believers truly believe are we able to be true to our nature and calling. The pastor's skills are not to primarily 'feed my giraffes' – by speaking over the heads of the sheep or to produce egg-heads, intellectuals who can debate and defeat every opposer of the faith – but to awaken greater confidence in the faithfulness of a God who invades and intervenes in the affairs of men and so justifies their faith in him.

I remember before I ever was a pastor, in fact soon after my conversion, complaining to the Lord that very few 'fish' were being caught, even though the first thing Jesus taught his followers was that he would make them catch men! (Mt. 4:19, 5:10) After my initial impact among my immediate family and friends, most of the potential catch of fish now seemed to swim off and get out of range. It was a revelation and releasing point in my controversy with the Lord when I suddenly realized that it was Jesus who had promised to make me a fisher of men, not that I should have the ability to make myself one. It was a promise, not a command, if I fulfilled the condition of following after him.

Faith, therefore, must be a prime objective in the pastor's agenda for his people. Consequently he must model it himself. The Lord has promised to make us catchers of fish. We must believe him and let him handle us and deal with us to get us where he wants us by his

Spirit. If we are going that way our church members will also follow.

2. GLOBAL VISION

Most sheep are parochial; they love looking in and not out. Something of this tendency is inevitable since it is necessary for each one of us to watch over our own souls to develop our own spiritual lives. We as pastors will have very little to give unless our own souls are healthy before the Lord. However, giving in to this preoccupation with ourselves and our own small interests generally leads to selfishness. Selfishness is the very thing Jesus came to save us from. 'If anyone wishes to come after me, let him deny himself, and take up his cross, and follow me' (Mk. 8:34). The next task therefore in the pastor's work-brief is to focus his people outwardly on to the world which we are here to serve. Often he will hear the plea of self-interest and be able to measure it by the proportion of the church income spent on ourselves rather than on world mission. Another complaint will be that we must major on building up home mission before we can think of the ends of the earth. However, Jesus said that it was a matter of *both* 'Jerusalem' *and* 'the ends of the earth'. I find it a continual and necessary duty to keep turning the flock outward. Hardly a Sunday passes without Matthew 24:14 being quoted: 'And this gospel of the kingdom shall be preached in the whole world for a witness to all the nations, and then the end shall come.' Added to this verse, news from workers in other countries is shared with the people. Of course, mission accomplished on the doorstep (Jerusalem) is essential to provide a resource from which to pour into the more distant world mission.

Home mission serves as an experience for training and inspiring new and developing workers to find their way eventually to the ends of the earth. World mission as a theoretical discussion, stance, or slogan should never be allowed to take the place of real front-line evangelism, so church planting at home is a necessity to keep our feet on the ground to fulfil the Great Commission. A discipleship programme therefore aimed at producing witnesses for world evangelism must be a subject high on the training agenda. A global perspective must result from our discipling the saints. To confine our attention to evangelizing our own nation only could still involve an element of selfishness; we would like more Christians in our home nation because it would make life easier and more agreeable to us. Home evangelism is to be done in the light of the global vision (Rev. 5:9,10).

3. THE HOLY SPIRIT

'You shall receive power after the Holy Spirit has come upon you' (Acts 1:8). The anointing of the Holy Spirit for witness and world evangelization is the essential ingredient for every believer. The Spirit of God precedes, stimulates, initiates and empowers witness so that, as in John 15, it is the Spirit who witnesses first (v.26) and then we the disciples (v.27). How important then to be moving with the Spirit so that our witnessing is in line with his and that he is taking the initiative in our lives. In fact it is the gift of the Spirit at Pentecost that seems absolutely vital to persuade the world to believe that a dead crucified carpenter in an obscure part of the Roman Empire two thousand years ago was the Son of God and has changed humanity's direction, and indeed its eternal destiny, and that the persistence of the world in unbelief concerning him is not just because there is not enough evidence, not just because there is not enough time, not just that we weren't brought up that way, but it is culpable sin.

'And he, when he comes, will convict the world concerning sin, and righteousness, and judgement; concerning sin, because they do not believe in me, and concerning righteousness, because I go to the Father, and you no longer behold me: and concerning judgement because the ruler of this world has been judged' (Jn. 16:8–11).

The pastor needs to be 100% convinced that not one of his flock can be an adequate witness without the Holy Spirit. In fact the four strands of New Testament material headed up by each of the four gospels all proclaim that the main reason for the Spirit's coming is to take the gospel to the world, and that without him this is impossible.

The first strand is the Jewish strand of Matthew, Hebrews and James. A representative from this strand of theology about the coming of the Spirit is Hebrews 2:3,4:

> ... so great a salvation ... first spoken through the Lord, it was confirmed to us by those who heard, God also bearing witness with them, both by signs and wonders and by various miracles, and by gifts of the Holy Spirit according to his own will.

The second strand is the Petrine: Mark (dictated by Peter), 1 and 2 Peter and Jude. 1 Peter 1:12 shows how Petrine theology understands the coming of the Spirit:

> It was revealed to them that they were not serving themselves, but you, in these things which now have been announced to you through those who preached the gospel to you by the Holy Spirit sent from heaven.

The third strand is Pauline: this comprises Luke/Acts and Paul's letters, since Luke was Paul's travelling companion. Luke 24:46–50 says:

> Thus it is written that the Christ should suffer and rise again from the dead on the third day; and that repentance for forgiveness of sins should be proclaimed in his name to all the nations, beginning from Jerusalem. You are witnesses of these things. And behold, I am sending forth the promise of my Father upon you; but you are to stay here in the city until you are clothed with power from on high.

Also 1 Corinthians 2:4 & 5

> And my message and my preaching were not in persuasive words of wisdom, but in demonstration of the Spirit and power that your faith should not rest on the wisdom of men, but on the power of God.

Finally the fourth strand of New Testament theology is

Johannine which of course is the gospel, letters and the Book of Revelation. John 16, which we have already noted, is representative of the Johannine emphasis:

> But I tell you the truth: it is to your advantage that I go away, for if I do not go away, the Helper shall not come to you; but if I go, I will send him to you. And he ... will convict the world concerning sin .... (Jn. 16:7,8).

All four strands of New Testament material confirm that the Spirit is given to the church, for the church to do the otherwise impossible task of world evangelization. The pastor himself must be Spirit-filled and able to minister the Spirit: 'Does he then, who provides you with the Spirit and works miracles among you, do it by the works of the Law, or by hearing with faith?' (Gal. 3:5). Over and above all the expertise required to help men and women to have reasons for the faith which lies within them (1 Pet. 3:15) the pastor also must continually work at the greatest argument of all, that of bringing the Spirit into people's lives. He must be able to teach the way of the Spirit for guidance and power. The main reason that the church was given the Spirit was for the fulfilment of the Great Commission. The church was not given a deluge of reasons or even apologetics in order to complete the Great Commission – they must be secondary: God's own presence by the Spirit comes first.

There are two complementary aspects of a witness. One is that of 'being good news' and the other is of 'speaking good news'.

Being Good News

To witness adequately the witness must be a person of integrity. In other words, he or she must be living a life which looks like good news in order to give substance to his word. Consequently, if priority is given to evangelistic techniques and programmes at the expense of developing Christ-like life there is little likelihood of a real advance.

Also it is not without significance that having called the disciples to catch men, Jesus sees the multitudes, goes up the mountainside and begins to teach the disciples that most wonderful lifestyle that the world has ever had presented to it – the Sermon on the Mount. He finishes this teaching in Matthew 5–7 with the parable of building on the rock of these truths – his words – and goes down the rocky mountain to the seashore of Galilee again to start showing the disciples how to catch fish. Lives built on the mount can be effective on the sand of the Galilean seashore for fishing.

In times of revival the temptation for the pastor has been to neglect the basic instruction concerning the Christ-like life. When the intensity of the Holy Spirit intuitively teaches the converts to adjust their lives and to abandon sinful ways more time must be given, thinks the pastor, to promoting the revival and providing meetings for seeking God, and exhausted pastors are devoid of the energy to continue to instruct the flock. Because the Spirit seems to inspire truth and obedience to witness, teaching the Bible seems perhaps irrelevant. The result has been invariably the loss of revival power, together with the falling away of the apparent converts. Whatever may be the divine reasons for heaven's ways in these matters is hardly the point of this short exhortation. The fact of the matter is that this is a reasonable interpretation of the observed pattern of the rise and decline of revivals.

The command of our Lord was to make disciples and teach them (Mt. 28:18–20). This must be done day in and day out, in season and out of season, as Paul would say to Timothy, (2 Tim. 4:2,5). We were commissioned to make and teach disciples whether revival is going on or not. We were not explicitly commissioned to carry revival to the world. That seems to be the Holy Spirit's job, as much as revival may help us, or be desirable. That is not exactly what our Great Commission mandate was; making, teaching and baptizing disciples is. Clearly the serious-minded committed pastor will teach his church to pray and prepare for and expect visitations from God (Acts

3:19), but the things commanded by our Lord will be his main concerns – to be pleasing to the one who ordains us into such a ministry.

Speaking Good News

With respect to the second area of evangelism, speaking the gospel, Matthew 4:14–23 shows us Jesus exercising what is known as proclamation evangelism: 'Repent for the kingdom of heaven is at hand' (Mt. 4:17), presence evangelism: 'Follow me, and I will make you fishers of men' (Mt. 4:19), and power evangelism: '[He travelled] throughout Galilee, teaching in their synagogues, and proclaiming the gospel of the kingdom, and healing every kind of disease and every kind of sickness among the people' (Mt. 4:23).

Whereas it has been helpful to divide evangelization into these three categories it is time for the church to be led into a comprehensive view of evangelism comprised of words, works and wonders. This is because each part requires the other two to give adequate testimony to Jesus. Half a testimony, or even worse, one third, can do more damage to a case in a court of law than no witnesses at all.

Presence evangelism is seen in this passage by the removal of Jesus' base of operations from Nazareth to Capernaum and was prophesied by Isaiah.

'This was to fulfil what was spoken through Isaiah the prophet, saying, "The land of Zebulun and the land of Naphtali, by the way of the sea, beyond the Jordan, Galilee of the Gentiles. The people who were sitting in darkness saw great light, and to those who were sitting in the land and shadow of death, upon them a light dawned"' (Mt. 4:14–16).

This action led to light shining into the darkness of ignorance, fear and death. All this took place before any preaching of Jesus is recorded. A worshipping, working community brings into secular society both the atmosphere of God's presence and the activity of Christ-like acts of care and concern. This is a witness which, as it is said, speaks louder than words – for such churches we thank God. However, if the heart is full of Christ, it is hard not to declare also his saving ability with the tongue.

'My heart is full of Christ and longs its glorious matter to declare' sings Charles Wesley. In our 'Jesus Action' programme, which reaches out largely to the deprived and disadvantaged, I have always found an opportunity to speak of Christ as well as to serve in his love. Perhaps I am just garrulous or have been too long too accustomed to preaching, but we must be examples to the flock in giving the greatest gift of love to people which is the knowledge of the salvation of our Christ. I personally find it difficult to pretend I am rendering loving services to them through good works if those good works are not interpreted by good words – words concerning the greatest love-gift of all.

Compassion which moves us to proclaim the good news by good works involves the knowledge of the great compassionate act of God. 'For God so loved the world, that he gave his only Son, so that everyone who believes in him may not perish but have eternal life' (Jn. 3:16). Works, words, presence and proclamation evangelism are one.

However, so too is power evangelism. Not only do signs and wonders confirm the work (Mk. 16:15–20), but are also part of the content of good news, the declaration that the kingdom is at hand.

'The Spirit of the Lord is upon me, because he anointed me to preach the gospel to the poor. He has sent me to proclaim release to the captives, and recovery of sight to the blind, to set free those who are down-trodden, to proclaim the favourable year of the Lord' (Lk. 4:18–19).

'And Jesus answered them, "Go and report to John what you hear and see: the blind receive sight, the lame walk, the lepers are cleansed, and the deaf hear, and the dead are raised, and the poor have the gospel preached to them"' (Mt. 11:4–5).

We bring 'good-news' to the world in power encounters. Again, however, it must be asked, 'How can signs stand on their own when it is promised they will confirm the word?' The words must come first to release the presence of signs and wonders. It is said of Jesus that he healed with a word (Mt. 8:8, Mk. 2:9–12) and also spoke in order to deliver the oppressed.

Word, wonders and indeed good works are all good ways to serve men and women but the task is achieved best when they are combined.

Total evangelism for the total world must come from a total church involvement. This requires total commitment of pastors to release their churches in the Holy Spirit to total comprehensive evangelism of which we must be models, mentors and motivators for mission, which is following Jesus into all the earth.

Releasing Good News

'March for Jesus' has involved 11 million believers around the world on one day. It is not just a means of proclamation, not just spiritual warfare, not just a good day out together or a demonstration of unity – it is all that – but also a means of moving our congregations from inside our church walls into exposure together to the world. The church of the streets – the only church Jesus knew – releases good news and releases those who participate into world evangelism.

The Last Word

'When he saw them he had compassion' (Mt. 9:36). The great motivation for our high calling as pastors is love to Christ, love from Christ, and the love of Christ to the world. Pastors, keep yourselves in the love of God and the world will know God so loved it that he gave his Son.

CHAPTER 2

The Dignity of the Pastoral Ministry

D. JOHN RICHARD

One of the purposes for which the Pastors Global Network of the AD2000 & Beyond Movement exists is: TO ENABLE THE PASTOR TO HAVE A GREATER UNDERSTANDING OF THE GRANDEUR AND DIGNITY OF THE MINISTRY ENTRUSTED TO HIM. This is all the more necessary because the world in which the church has to function has scant regard for the pastoral ministry. That, however, is not surprising. Should not the servant go the way of the master? Jesus has taught us: 'You shall be hated of all men for my name's sake ... The disciple is not above his master, nor the servant above his lord. It is enough for the disciple that he be as his master, and the servant as his lord' (Mt. 10:22,24–25). Jesus was 'despised and rejected of men; a man of sorrows, and acquainted with grief' (Isa. 53:3). It is sad to see the servant of the one who came to give his life for the ungodly (Rom. 5:6), for sinners (Rom. 5:8), and for his enemies (Rom. 5:10) ignored and often ridiculed.

It is sadder to observe that even the Christian community, which ought to have a better understanding of pastoral work, treats it no better. To many Christians the medical or engineering professions, for instance, occupy a higher rung on the ladder of status. (The Korean pastor, however, is an exception. He is held in high regard by his church members.) In several economically deprived countries, when a Christian young person does not make his mark in any other field, he is often shunted off by his parents to the pastoral ministry for the sake of getting some material benefit such as a rent-free parsonage.

It is the saddest of all, however, when the pastor himself has a poor self-image. It is biblical to have a low opinion of oneself. It is biblical for the pastor to remember that God can use in his service only those with whom his glory is safe (1 Cor. 1:29). It is quite biblical for the pastor to pray what a Puritan of a former generation prayed: 'O Lord, open Thou mine eyes that I might see the real smallness of my greatest greatness.' But that is not what we are referring to. We are concerned that many a pastor has a deficient understanding of the grandeur of the ministry entrusted to him. We hope that this little book will remedy that to some extent. Not only that, we pray that some committed lay Christians may embrace the ranks of the pastoral ministry as they ponder over its excellence.

We will treat this topic, THE DIGNITY OF THE PASTORAL MINISTRY, under five different headings:

1. As depicted in its divine origin
2. As depicted in its glory
3. As depicted in its greatness
4. As depicted in its nature and purpose
5. As depicted in its reward

THE DIGNITY OF THE PASTORAL MINISTRY
AS DEPICTED IN ITS DIVINE ORIGIN

(a) It is the Father Who Has Given Us the Ministry

In 2 Chronicles 29, we read of the Levites purifying the temple. They give heed to the exhortations of the good king Hezekiah who calls upon them to consecrate themselves and also the temple of the Lord. He instructs them to remove all filthiness from the sanctuary and then counsels them: 'My sons, be not now negligent: for the Lord has chosen you to stand before him, to serve him, and burn incense' (2 Chron. 29:11). Or, as the New International Version has it: 'My sons, do not be negligent now, for the LORD has chosen you to stand before him and serve him, to minister before him and to burn incense.' It is an honour indeed that the Lord has chosen us to stand in the presence of the Lord even as he chose the angel Gabriel to stand in his presence. We recollect how Gabriel introduced himself to Zechariah, the priest, in Luke 1:19. But we are also those chosen to minister to him and to serve as his ministers. Again we are like the mighty angels of the Lord who, as they are depicted in Psalm 103, do his word, listening to the voice of his word. God has given us this high privilege of first ministering joy and satisfaction to his heart, and then burning incense to him, that is, as priests interceding with him on behalf of our people, since we have been given the ministry of intercession. But to us has also been given the ministry of reconciliation. The apostle Paul declares: 'God . . . gave us the ministry of reconciliation' (2 Cor. 5:18 (NIV)), or 'God has given us the privilege of urging everyone to come into his favour and be reconciled to him' (2 Cor. 5:18 (TLB)).

That is, we are to cooperate with God in reconciling the world to himself. The peoples of this world are alienated from God and they have to be reinstated in his favour. Towards this end you and I as pastors have a crucial role to fulfil. As servants of the church, our chief task is to proclaim the whole counsel of God. 'I have become the servant of the church by the commission God gave me to present to you the word of God in all its fulness' (Col. 1:25).

(b) It is the Son of God Who Has Commissioned Us for the Ministry

The charge of the risen Lord to his disciples was: 'As the Father has sent me, so I send you' (Jn. 20:21). The Lord elevates this commission to the level of the commission he himself had received from the Father God. What Christ bids us do, he certainly will enable us to do. The apostle Paul affirms: 'He who calls you is faithful, and he will do it' (1 Thess. 5:24).

Because he has sent us, we can do all things that he intends to accomplish through us.

The apostle Paul claims: 'I can do everything through him who gives me strength' (Phil. 4:13). Archbishop Sir Marcus Loane paraphrases this passage: 'I am strong to do and bear all things by virtue of my union with Christ who never ceases to make me able.'

The secret is our union with Christ. David Gracey, a Bible teacher of a former generation, describes this UNION as:

i.   A union of support: He is the foundation; we are the building (Eph. 2:19–22).
ii. A union of sustenance: He is the vine; we are the branches (Jn. 15:5).
iii. A union of guardianship: He is the shepherd; we are the flock (Jn. 10:11).
iv. A union of kindred: He is the elder brother and we are the family (Rom. 8:16–17).
v.   A union of love: He is the husband; we are the bride (Eph. 5:32).
vi. A union of life: He is the head and we are the members of his body (Eph. 1:22–23).

(c) It is the Holy Spirit Who Has Appointed Us to Our Ministry

It is a permanent appointment. We cannot quit his service at any time we wish. Neither is it a job whose working hours are regulated. We have no trade union rights. We cannot tell God or our people that we will be pastors for just eighteen hours a day and that the remaining six hours are for our use according to our good pleasure.

In his charge to the Ephesian elders the apostle Paul warned: 'Take heed to yourselves and to all the flock over which the Holy Spirit has appointed you guardians, to shepherd the church, that is, tend and feed and guide the church of the Lord God which he obtained for himself buying it and saving it (for himself) – with his own blood' (Acts 20:28, ANT).

Part of this 'taking heed', part of this personal watchfulness requires that we, who are in this business of feeding others with the bread of life, do not starve ourselves. And what a terrible tragedy it would be if we seek to build up others when we ourselves are spiritually lean. Why has the Holy Spirit appointed us as guardians of the flock? Surely, it is in order that the people in our care may reflect the beauty, the mind and the character of Christ. Jesus said: 'When the Holy Spirit comes, he shall glorify me' (Jn. 16:14). That is the chief office of the Holy Spirit. That is his continuing ministry. And by what better means than the pastoral ministry can this be done? This is a ministry given to us by God the Father, to which we have been commissioned by God the Son and to which we have been appointed by God the Holy Spirit.

THE DIGNITY OF THE PASTORAL MINISTRY
AS DEPICTED IN ITS GLORY

The glory of our ministry is based on three great facts:

a) It lies in the glory of the one whom we serve.
b) It lies in the weakness of the instruments whom God uses.
c) It lies in the expendability of the ones who serve Christ.

a) The glory of our ministry lies in the glory of the one whom we serve. He is THE INCARNATE ONE. He is the one who is fully God and fully man. He is the one of whom alone it can be said: GOD, WITHOUT CEASING TO BE GOD, BECAME MAN. He is THE CRUCIFIED ONE. He is the one who died for our sins according to the Scriptures. He is the one who himself bore our sins in his body on the tree, so that we might die to sins and live for righteousness. He is THE RESURRECTED ONE. He is the one who rose from the dead according to the Scriptures, the one who was not abandoned to the grave. He is the one who brought about the death of death, the one who has promised us: 'Because I live, you shall live also.' He is THE ASCENDED ONE. He is the one who was taken up to heaven before the very eyes of the apostles. He is the one of whom two white-robed men told the apostles: 'Men of Galilee, why are you standing here staring at the sky? Jesus has gone away to heaven, and some day, just as he went, he will return' (Acts 1:11). He is THE EXALTED ONE, the one who has been exalted to the right hand of God; the one whose ascension and exaltation has produced the outpouring of God's Spirit upon his waiting church; the one who has been exalted to the highest place and given a name which is above every other name. He is THE INTERCEDING ONE, our ever-living intercessor who is even now at the right hand of God interceding for us. He is the one who through his priestly ministry is able to save completely all those who go to God through him. He is THE RETURN-ING SAVIOUR. 'Just as he went up to heaven, so will he return.' He is the one who will come down from heaven with a mighty shout and with the soul-stirring cry of the archangel and the great trumpet call of God. He is the one with whom we want to stay in happy fellowship so that when he appears we may be confident and unashamed before him at his coming.

Yes, he is THE INCARNATE, CRUCIFIED, RES-URRECTED, ASCENDED, EXALTED, INTERCEDING and RETURNING SAVIOUR. And the glory of our ministry lies in the glory of the one whom we serve.

b) The second great fact in which the glory of our ministry lies is the weakness of the instruments which God uses. That our great God should condescend to use even us is a truth that humbles us. Who are we that he should want to use us as his instruments? Especially when the angels of heaven, the winds and the seas and all nature are ready to spring to instant obedience at his bidding! We are mere worms, creatures of the earth, but then we are the Lord's worms. Herein lies the glory of our ministry. Isaiah gives us this word of assurance: ' "Do not be afraid, O worm Jacob, O little Israel, for I myself will help you," declares the LORD, your Redeemer, the Holy One of Israel' (41:14). Yes, we are worms, fit to be trodden upon, fit to be despised and cast onto the dung heap as unwanted garbage. But then Isaiah gives us a further word of promise in v.15: 'See, I will make you into a threshing sledge, new and sharp, with many teeth. You will thresh the mountain and crush them and reduce the hills to chaff.' From mere worms to mighty sledges, sledges that will crush the mountains of unbelief and dislodge the hills of doubt and difficulty.

Our God has been in the business of converting worms into threshing sledges ever since man populated the earth. Nor has he confined himself to the use of humans alone. Things insignificant, things that the world will dismiss as nonentities, these our great God has used in the furtherance of his purposes. God uses weak instruments in order to accomplish great purposes. This is a recurring theme throughout the Scriptures. A staff in the hand of Moses became a venomous snake. With the jaw-bone of an ass, Samson struck down a thousand Philistines. With just a sling and a stone, David felled Goliath, that towering giant. In a time of drought and famine, the widow of Zarephath found that her jar of flour was not used up and her jug of oil did not run dry. The widow, her family and Elijah were miraculously sustained day by day. A cloud as small as a man's hand became heavy rain-bearing clouds. The mustard seed is the smallest of all seeds. When it grows it becomes a big tree affording lodging to the birds of the air. Five small barley loaves and two small fish in the hands of a boy were multiplied to feed five thousand people and have twelve full baskets left over.

This manner of God's dealings is true also when it comes to the edification and enriching of the church. Divine truth has been deposited in the pastoral ministry as treasure in earthen vessels. The apostle Paul says: '. . . we possess this precious treasure, the divine light of the gospel, in frail, human vessels of earth, that the grandeur and exceeding greatness of the power may be shown to be of God and not from ourselves' (2 Cor. 4:7 ANT). Almighty strength is made perfect in weakness in order that no flesh should glory in his presence. Once Francis of Assisi was asked why God chose him to be his messenger. His response was, 'God knew that his glory would be safe with me.'

c) The third great fact in which the glory of our ministry lies is the expendability of the ones who serve Christ. We are expendable members of the army of the Lord. We are at the disposal of our heavenly Commander. If he wants to station us in the front-line, where we will be exposed to death and destruction, we will gladly be so. It may cost us our lives but never the progress of the gospel. If he wants to post us in some obscure hard place, where we may have to labour for years without seeing any visible fruit, that, too, we will readily do. We know that others in due course will reap the fruit of our labour. If he wants to place us in the midst of a congregation, who will treat us as the scum of the earth and as the refuse of the world, we will give our glad consent. We are his property and he has every right to deal with us as he wishes. And in the total abandonment of Christ's servants to God's purposes lies the glory of our ministry.

THE DIGNITY OF THE PASTORAL MINISTRY
AS DEPICTED IN ITS GREATNESS

More specifically, the greatness of our ministry is seen in:

a)   God's sovereign choice of us
b)   God's gracious need for us
c)   God's generous provision for us

a) First, the greatness of our ministry is seen in God's sovereign choice of us. 'The ministry is the choicest of his choice, the elect of his election, a church picked out of his church.' So said a saint of a former generation. That is perhaps the highest tribute one can pay to the pastoral ministry. It identifies the pastor as one who has been picked out by God himself to be his personal representative. This sovereign choice should cause us to give a two-fold solemn response. Firstly, it will be one of profound, deep gratitude. That he should have by-passed a thousand others and chosen you and me to represent his heavenly court here in this ungodly world is a blessed honour indeed. Upon us has been conferred a dignity of no small worth. Secondly, it will be to represent God in a manner worthy of his name. Unlike any earthly ambassador, we are called to represent our king with our whole being. We belong to him from the crown of our head to the sole of our feet. We are, therefore, to serve him with our body, mind and spirit. What goes forth from our mouths should be backed up by our daily living. Our deeds should be in line with our doctrine, our conduct with our creed and our behaviour with our beliefs. What we say and what we do should go hand in hand. Then we will follow in the footsteps of our LORD of whom it is said: 'The LORD visited Sarah as he had said, and the LORD did to Sarah as he had spoken' (Gen. 21:1). When our words and deeds agree, that will be a double confirmation that our credentials are from the Court of Heaven. The greatness of our ministry is seen in God's sovereign choice of us.

b) Second, the greatness of our ministry is seen in God's gracious need for us. We are not those who merely work for God. We are those who also work with God. What more! We are those with whom God works. Paul has this in mind when he refers to us as fellow-workers with God.

We are joint promoters and labourers together with God. Both individually and collectively we are fellow-workers with God. This aspect of collective involvement needs to be engraved upon our hearts. Especially in these days when there is an increasing tendency to engage in solo performance; when there is so much jealousy and backbiting and fighting and quarrelling even among ministerial colleagues, we need to remember afresh the words of the apostle Paul: 'What, after all, is Apollos? And what is Paul? Only servants, through whom you came to believe – as the Lord has assigned to each his task. I planted the seed, Apollos watered it, but God made it grow. So neither he who plants nor he who waters is anything but only God who makes things grow' (1 Cor. 3:5–7).

The one who plants is nothing. The one who waters is nothing. It is ridiculous that two nothings should fight one against the other. This shameful bickering is nothing but a sordid advertisement of the presence of carnality in our hearts. And the mind of the flesh with its carnal thoughts is hostile to God.

Yes, the man who plants is nothing and the man who waters is nothing. True, they are nothing when it comes to imparting life. But then they are something when it comes to nurturing life. So, pastors, we are something after all. And the greatness of the pastoral ministry is that the God who is the life-giver should seek our services as the life-nourisher. He could have easily dispensed with our services. He could have fed and fattened the souls of our people directly through the ministrations of the Holy Spirit. But he has chosen deliberately to make himself dependent on us. In a sense, he has cast himself on us to see that we do not fail him in the acts of planting and watering. It is not surprising that Paul calls us fellow-workers with God.

God's gracious need for us is also seen in the fact that pastors are given as one of the gifts by the ascended Christ to the Church. In Ephesians 4:11–12 we read that Christ gave some to be apostles, some to be prophets, some to be evangelists, and some to be pastors and teachers to prepare God's people for works of service, so that the body of Christ may be built up. Pastors, teachers and evangelists enjoy the same ranking as apostles and prophets because of their common end purpose, namely, the building up of the body of Christ.

God needs us as his fellow-workers. He needs us to do our part in the building up of the body of Christ. He needs us, too, as kings and priests. Revelation 1:6 teaches us that God has made us kings and priests to himself. As kings, we take of the things of God and distribute them to his people. To speak on behalf of God is a task that not even angels can do. Experience is a pre-requisite to communication. Only he who has experienced the saving power of Christ can communicate what it means to possess this experience.

> Never did angels taste above,
> Redeeming grace and dying love.

Thus, we have the honour of going to man on behalf of God. But we also have the honour of going to God on behalf of man. As priests, we can freely enter into partnership with the praying Christ; we can take to God the concerns and burdens of our people in the name of the interceding Christ.

c) Third, the greatness of our ministry is seen in God's generous provision for us.

God does not call us to serve him without adequately equipping us to do so. And his generous provision includes Christ as our leader, the Holy Spirit as our enabler, the word of God as our instructor and the blood of Christ as our purifier.

Christ himself is our leader in our warfare against the evil one and the demonic forces. He is the captain of our salvation, the risen Lord who defeated the prince of this world on the cross of Calvary. Having disarmed the principalities and the powers ranged against us by openly triumphing over them in the cross, he has now become head over every power and authority. It is this Christ whom we serve. In every situation in which we find ourselves, he is there already.

God's generous provision includes also the Holy Spirit as our enabler. 'But you will receive power when the Holy Spirit comes on you: and you will be my witnesses in Jerusalem, and in all Judea and Samaria and to the ends of the earth' (Acts 1:8). You will receive power, that is, ability, efficiency and might. 'Not by might, nor by power, but by my Spirit, says the LORD Almighty' (Zech. 4:6). The Holy Spirit is well able to equip us with spiritual power even as he did Stephen and Paul and the apostles of old.

Next, God's generous provision for us includes the word of God as our instructor. What are our personal needs and the needs of our church members? Are these a fresh revelation of Jesus in times of doubt and dismay, or spiritual refreshment in times of dryness and barrenness, or spiritual strength in times of powerlessness in service, or comfort in times of sorrow, or guidance, and light in times of perplexity? For all these and more than these, the written word of God is there to instruct and enlighten us. Can we possibly conceive of our ministry without the Bible in our hand or its precious promises hidden in our heart?

Furthermore, God's generous provision for us includes the blood of Christ as our purifier. The blood of Jesus, God's son, purifies us from every sin (1 Jn. 1:7b). We are serving Christ in a fallen world. We are prone to contamination by sin. But God has taken care of this, too. Jesus' blood goes on cleansing us moment by moment, provided of course that we learn never to graduate from the foot of the cross; provided of course that we keep on looking to Jesus for his continual cleansing. Such a cleansing avails us as we keep short accounts with God and with our people through repentance and confession of our sins. Then we will be able to stand at our full height and look straight into the eyes of our fellow beings with no accusing finger troubling our conscience.

God's choice of us, his need for us and his provision for us are three components that make our ministry great. Our salary may be small but our job is big. We serve no earthly employer; we serve Jesus Christ, King of kings and Lord of lords. Small wonder, therefore, that Philip Henry could make that triumphant declaration: 'I take you all to record that a life spent in the service of Christ is the happiest life that a man can spend upon earth.'

THE DIGNITY OF THE PASTORAL MINISTRY
AS DEPICTED IN ITS NATURE AND PURPOSE

What is the nature of the pastoral ministry? The answer is embedded in the question itself. It is pastoral, it is shepherding of all the flock. Not some of the flock, but all of the flock, caring for every member of the flock.

One of the key Scriptures highlighting this truth is Acts 20:28 (a Scripture we have already referred to), part of Paul's farewell speech to the Ephesian elders. He exhorts: 'Take heed, therefore, to yourselves and to all the flock, over which the Holy Spirit has made you overseers, to feed the church of God, which he has purchased with his own blood.'

The nature of our pastoral work is supremely shepherding, that is, to follow the example of our Lord Jesus Christ, whom the New Testament describes as the good shepherd, the great shepherd and the chief shepherd. Like him we are to have a heart pulsating with love that is prepared to die for the sake of the flock. Like him we are to have a special eye for those wandering away from the fold. Like him we are to show a faithfulness that will not desert the sheep in times of danger. Like him we are to exert strength to rescue sheep from the mouth of marauding animals. Like him we are to manifest a tender heart for the young, the weak and the struggling sheep.

In short, shepherding involves giving of ourselves and our lives for them; seeking the straying sheep, whether they do so through ignorance or through wantonness. Further, shepherding involves carrying the lambs, as it were, in our arms, applying the balm of the gospel to their distressed souls and tending and mending their broken lives. Moreover shepherding involves leading the sheep to the green pastures of God's word and feeding them with food that fosters spiritual growth; and, above all, watching over them and sheltering them from the wiles of the devil.

In practice this will mean, firstly, that we work hard for the conversion of the unconverted; that we do not conclude anyone to be a true believer unless we see the evidence of salvation in that person's life. Secondly, that we make ourselves available to counsel at any and every time those who approach us with troubled consciences. Thirdly, that we build up those whose lives do not reflect like mirrors the glory and the grace of the Lord Jesus Christ; those who as yet have not been delivered from those besetting sins which are frequently tripping them up in their Christian walk; those who have backslidden and have lost their first love for the Lord Jesus Christ. Fourthly, that we care for our families which are breaking up under the onslaught of the craze for sex, the desire to possess everything that appeals to the eye and the pride that comes from position, prestige and wealth. Fifthly, that we visit the sick and help them to prepare for whatever God has in store for them. If a new lease of life were to be given, then we are to ensure that this extended life is invested for the service of God; or, if death is to be the portion, to prepare that soul for an abundant and happy entrance to heaven. Sixthly, we are to solemnly warn those who are unrepentant and continue sinning with delight, of the awful end that awaits them. Seventhly and lastly, we should not hesitate to exercise church discipline after all avenues of restoration have been fully explored.

Now let us dwell briefly on the purpose of our ministry although its nature and purpose are so closely intertwined, that it is difficult to make a sharp distinction between them. <u>What is the end purpose of our pastoral</u> <u>ministry?</u> The answer, we believe, is found in Colossians 1:28. The apostle Paul says: 'We proclaim Christ, admonishing and teaching everyone with all wisdom, so that we may present everyone perfect in Christ.' What does this expression 'perfect in Christ' mean? Christ is the element in whom every believer moves and has his being. It is in Christ that every believer can find perfection, that is, become fully instructed in doctrine and fully mature in faith and practice. Paul's concern is that every believer would be presented at Christ's coming perfect in Christ. In order to accomplish this, Paul says, he proclaims Christ accompanied by the twin responsibilities of admonishing and teaching. Admonishing or warning is intended to produce right behaviour through repentance and is addressed primarily to the heart. Teaching on the other hand is intended to produce right beliefs through faith and is addressed primarily to the intellect. And the target audience of this two-fold exercise is everyone, with no selectivity, no exemption. This exercise is directed with all wisdom, wisdom that is from above.

But then this end purpose of presenting everyone perfect in Christ has to be supported and furthered by several other related purposes. All these constitute the purpose of our pastoral ministry. To us is given the honour of serving as the mirror or conveyor of God's truth to people groping about in spiritual darkness; of facing the enemies of truth and of contending for the faith that God gave once for all to keep without change through the years. To comfort the disturbed; to disturb the comforted; to edify the saints; to disclose the mysteries of heaven; to bear patiently with those who wilfully delight in doing evil; to guide those whose values of life are distorted — all these are no ordinary undertakings. To us has been given the privilege, too, of hastening the return of our Lord Jesus Christ. God is at work through his messengers, taking out of all nations a people for his name. The body of Christ on earth is being completed day by day. And one day this work of completion will end and then 'the Lord himself will descend from heaven with a loud cry of summons, with the shout of an archangel and with the blast of the trumpet of God. And those who have departed this life in Christ will rise first. Then we the still living who remain (on the earth), shall simultaneously be caught up along with (the resurrected dead) in the clouds to meet the Lord in the air; and so always – through the eternity of the eternities – we shall be with the Lord' (1 Thess. 4:16–17). Until then, as shepherds of the flock, we are to go about our duties diligently and faithfully, as Christ's mighty energy continues to work in us.

THE DIGNITY OF THE PASTORAL MINISTRY
AS DEPICTED IN ITS REWARD

As we press forward in our pastoral ministry, there is a reward that becomes our portion both now and in the hereafter. God is not like some of us who during a person's life-time have little or no compliments to offer but who heap encomiums on him when he lies dead. On the contrary, God is a great encourager. Just because he is that, he has filled his word with many precious promises, promises that urge us to greater obedience and greater victories in our spiritual pursuits. Here is a promise from the one who never alters that which goes out of his mouth, a promise to be appropriated by faith for our present comfort: 'For I am the LORD, your God, who takes hold of your right hand and says to you, "Do not fear; I will help you"' (Isa. 41:13). Here is a promise for our protection in times of danger: "'Don't be afraid", the prophet answered, "Those who are with us are more than those who are with them"' (2 Ki. 6:16). Here is a promise of strength when we are weak: 'So do not fear, for I am with you; do not be dismayed, for I am your God. I will strengthen and help you. I will uphold you with my righteous right hand' (Isa. 41:10). Yet another promise of his presence with us in our times of trouble: 'When you pass through the waters, I will be with you: and when you pass through the rivers, they will not sweep over you. When you walk through the fire, you will not be burned; the flames will not set you ablaze' (Isa. 43:2).

So we may go on. But the reward that we have is not

just that of leaning on the invisible God by faith. More specifically, we are thinking of the joys that we experience in the here-and-now as we see souls who have been given over to sin and selfishness renouncing them, being established in the faith and incorporated into the church.

How greatly our souls rejoice when, for example, we hear a converted Hindu woman testify: 'I sweep the floor cleaner, I cook my husband's food better. I talk to him mildly when he gets angry. I show him that Christ has made me a better wife.' Not surprising, therefore, if before long her husband puts his saving faith in Christ. That is an enactment of what the apostle Peter has stated: 'Wives, . . . be submissive to your husbands so that, if any of them do not believe the word, they may be won over without talk by the behaviour of their wives' (1 Pet. 3:1). Mark the words: WON OVER WITHOUT TALK. When husbands are won over to the Lord not by words piled on words but by the godly lives of their wives surely that is a high tribute to the pastors and other messengers whom God has used in relating these wives to Jesus Christ and his life-changing gospel. Nor are we thinking merely of the joy that is ours when we see people becoming new creations in Christ Jesus; the joy that is ours when we take pains to seek the spiritual welfare of all our flock. There is also a comforting joy in knowing that we are doing ourselves spiritual good whenever we share God's word and his blessed gospel with others who are strangers to his saving grace. We read in Ezekiel 3:18–19: 'When I say to a wicked man, "you will surely die," and you do not warn him or speak out to dissuade him from his evil ways in order to save his life, that wicked man will die for his sin, and I will hold you accountable for his blood. But if you do warn the wicked man and he does not turn from his wickedness or from his evil ways, he will die for his sin, but you will have saved yourself.' You will have saved yourself. You will have done good to yourself. This good that accrues to us is a reason for our present joy. But the greater reason for our joy and satisfaction is to see the increase of the glory of the King of saints, especially as saints are added to his family through our labours. When God uses us to enhance the numerical and spiritual growth of the church, it is his own glory that is enhanced. This is our chief source of joy and that, too, is a reward of immeasurable worth.

But then this joy has a dimension that extends beyond our present life. The Lord Jesus Christ concluded the parable of the 'wheat and tares' with the words: 'The Son of man will send out his angels, and they will weed out of his kingdom everything that causes sin and all who do evil. They will throw them into the fiery furnace, where there will be weeping and gnashing of teeth. Then the righteous will shine like the sun in the kingdom of their Father' (Mt. 13:41–43). A time comes when those who are upright and in right standing with God through Jesus Christ will shine forth as the sun in the kingdom of their Father. This noble company includes Christ's servants and those whom they have led to receive the gift of salvation. In the book of Daniel it is said that during the end times: 'Those who are wise will shine like the brightness of the sky, and those who lead many to righteousness, like the stars forever and ever' (Dan. 12:3). Those who are wise or those who impart wisdom will shine like the brightness of the sky. And who are the wise? In Proverbs 11:30 we read: 'He who wins souls is wise.' The wisdom of the philosopher, the scholar or the statesman comes nowhere near the wisdom that leads a soul to Christ. To shine like the sun and the stars forever and ever is the joyful prospect before us.

Not just this prospect alone. To us will be given varied crowns. First, when the Chief Shepherd appears, we will receive the CROWN OF GLORY that will never fade away (1 Pet. 5:4). This is something special for Christ's under-shepherds. Second, we will receive the CROWN OF RIGHTEOUSNESS reserved for all those who long for his appearing. 'Now there is in store for me the crown of righteousness, which the Lord, the righteous Judge, will award to me on that day' (2 Tim. 4:8). Third, there is the CROWN OF LIFE to those who are patient in trial and stand up under temptation. James 1:12 says: 'Blessed is the man who perseveres under trial, because when he has stood the test he will receive the crown of life that God has promised to those who love him.' Fourth, there is the INCORRUPTIBLE CROWN. The apostle Paul writes: 'Now every athlete who goes into training conducts himself temperately and restricts himself in all things. They do it to win a wreath that will soon wither but we do it to receive a crown of eternal blessedness, a crown that will not wither away' (1 Cor. 9:25). All these crowns become our portion and the portion of those in whose lives Jesus has come to reign through our endeavours. But then let us hold fast to that which we have lest someone take our crown (Rev. 3:11).

Jesus Christ is coming soon. Until then may we conduct ourselves in a manner worthy of the dignity with which our pastoral ministry has been invested. God's servants down through the years have been keenly conscious of the honour that has been conferred on them. So we are not surprised when Mr Scott exclaims: 'With all my discouragements and sinful despondency; in my better moments I can think of no work worth doing compared to this. Had I a thousand lives, I would willingly spend them in it; and had I as many sons, I should gladly devote them to it.' Cotton Mather once told those entering the ministry: 'You are entering upon a work that will keep you continually in the way of this incomparable satisfaction, and I hope that the saving or enlightening and edifying of one soul at any time will be a matter of more joy unto you than if all the wealth of Ophir should flow in upon you.' Pastors, we serve the Lord Christ.

To him be the glory for ever and ever! Amen!

CHAPTER 3

The Story of Emmanuel Methodist Church, Madras, India

REVD DR MARTIN ALPHONSE

Senior Pastor (Until June '94)
& District Superintendent.

The Emmanuel Methodist Church, popularly known as EMC, is a unit of the Methodist Church in India. Centrally located at the heart of Madras, a mega-city of India, EMC has been well-recognized as an outstanding evangelical and evangelistic church. EMC has been so dedicated to evangelism that it has planted as many as 12 'daughter-churches' in the past ten years, as well as being currently involved in planting another four. Each newly-planted church has an average membership of about 75 adults, most of whom are fresh converts from other religions. In addition, each congregation has an average of about 30 children and youth placed on the roll of preparatory membership. The story of how EMC has been able to carry out successfully its church-planting ministry is interesting to tell. Several factors have contributed to making EMC an outstanding evangelistic church.

SOUND BIBLICAL TEACHING

EMC was planted in 1878 as a result of a series of evangelistic meetings held in the city by William Taylor, an American evangelist. The church had been growing slowly since that time. Something remarkable happened in the 1950s during the ministry of the Revd Schneck, a missionary pastor of the church, when, it is reported, the pastor underwent a conversion experience during a special evangelistic service conducted by an evangelist at the church. The Revd Schneck himself responded to the altar call given by the evangelist one evening. Subsequently the congregation began to witness a radical change in the pastor's sermons. The Revd Schneck began the tradition of sound biblical teaching from the pulpit, which has since been valued, cherished and maintained as a heritage. EMC has always been known as 'a church with a strong pulpit'.

STRONG PASTORAL LEADERSHIP

The Revd Dr Samuel Kamaleson succeeded the Revd Schneck as the first national pastor of EMC. Kamaleson was himself a gifted evangelist. While continuing sound biblical preaching from the pulpit he also regularly preached evangelistic sermons which in the next 13 years of his pastoral ministry had brought a number of people, especially the youth, to Christ. His passion for evangelism had an influence on the congregation, as a result of which it is reported that as many as 35 persons responded to God's call for full-time Christian service in the 13 years of his ministry at EMC, some of them resigning lucrative careers for the sake of preaching the gospel. The trend continues on, with an average of at least 2 students from EMC being sponsored for theological studies every year, and others resigning from their professions to enter into full-time Christian service. By the grace of God, almost all the pastors who have served in succession to this day, have kept the evangelistic zeal and fervour growing among the members of the congregation. They have constantly maintained evangelism as the heartbeat of EMC.

A SYSTEMATIC OUTREACH PROGRAMME

The Revd Stanley Downes (who later was elected as a Bishop) moved to EMC as senior pastor in 1975. Just about that time, a team of laity from the church had inaugurated a church-planting outreach ministry in a suburban village called Pudur, about 20 miles west of Madras. As soon as the Revd Downes assumed leadership at EMC, he decided to systematize and consolidate the Pudur evangelistic project. A theologically trained graduate was appointed as resident evangelist of Pudur in 1976. It took two years before a Hindu couple was baptized as the first fruits. In the next three years a church was organized with about 40 members. A primary school which was started in 1974 to cater for the educational needs of the poor began to flourish. Encouraged by the results of Pudur, EMC launched church planting ministries in other unreached villages.

EMC's evangelistic methodology in the initial stages had been as follows:

1. A team of lay people, comprising both men and women, would go to a chosen village on Sunday afternoons. They would do open-air preaching, tract distribution and visit house to house. Depending upon the response, the team would continue visiting the village every Sunday afternoon for several consecutive weeks.
2. A theologically trained graduate with spiritual gifts in evangelism would then be appointed as resident evangelist. The evangelist would continue with the personal ministry as well as meeting families as a group. Eventually a handful of people would be

baptized and would form the nucleus of the church. Normally in the space of two years about 30 adults would be baptized and a church formed.

3. Normally women and youth respond to the gospel more enthusiastically than men. Hence meeting them is given priority, without, of course, neglecting the men altogether. Baptism of individuals is delayed until a few more members or, if possible, the entire family is ready to be baptized.

4. There has been a change in the modus operandi in the last 10 years. On the one hand, the lay people's team began to slow down on their regular Sunday outreach visits due to other commitments. On the other hand, more theologically trained candidates keep applying for positions as evangelists and church-planters. They are straightaway appointed to an outreach centre. A team of lay people do visit the centre regularly in order to encourage and assist the evangelist in his pioneer work. For instance, there are two slum areas in Madras city, one visited regularly by a team of Methodist Men, and the other by a team of the Women's Society of Christian Service. Both these places are growing gradually.

MOTIVATION AND MOBILIZATION OF THE LAITY

The Missions and Evangelism Committee of EMC consists of men and women gifted in the area of evangelism. They are deeply committed to making Christ known in as many places as possible. By the general counsel and constant encouragement of the pastor, the Missions and Evangelism Committee holds a 'Mission Sunday Service' on the fifth Sundays. This happens 4 times a year. The 'Mission Sunday' is meant to motivate, mobilize and intensify the involvement of the laity in evangelism. Extended seasons of fasting and prayer for Mission and Evangelism are a regular and a well-attended programme on these Mission Sundays.

EMPHASIS ON MISSION-GIVING

Over 37% of the Church's budget is designated for
Mission and Evangelism in one way or another. It takes
care of the monthly salary of the outreach evangelists, or
provides a substantial grant to some of the outreach
centres. In addition, EMC is also partially supporting
missionaries of three indigenous mission organizations.
About 5 mission agencies are given a one-time grant
annually. EMC pays the largest amount apportioned for
the Home Mission Project of the Methodist Church. It is a
project that covers the subsidy for a number of pastors
and evangelists appointed to remote hamlets and villages
in the neighbouring states. The laity are taught stewardship and encouraged to invest their financial resources in
evangelism. The response has always been enthusiastic.

CONCLUSION

In the past twenty years, the Emmanuel Methodist
Church has mothered twelve daughter churches within
Madras city. It has also 'adopted' four infant churches
planted by the Bethel Agricultural Fellowship, Danishpet,
Salem, located about 250 miles south of Madras. These
four churches are growing rapidly. About 100 adults
converted from non-christian religions were baptized in
these churches during 1992–93. Mass baptism has
become a recurring phenomenon in this region. The
pastors and members of EMC are determined to keep on
planting more churches in the future, thus continuing
faithfully with the heritage they have received. Their
enthusiasm is simply inexhaustible. It will, hopefully,
never end.

The secret behind this continuing success story emerges
out of the biblical vision affirmed in Proverbs 29:18:
'Where there is no vision people perish.' EMC stubbornly
refuses to let people perish. Hence evangelism has become
its passion and obsession. It is willing to stretch itself to

any length and is willing to expand its horizons of evangelistic involvement to any extent, all for the sake of the glory and the name of our Lord Jesus Christ, and in obedience to his Great Commission. When the passion for evangelism dies, EMC may die. But EMC has strongly determined to live on while waiting patiently for the return of our Lord. Hence evangelism will continue to be the success story of EMC until that glorious day of his coming again.

CHAPTER 4

The Indian Model
The Evangelical Church Of India
(A Success Story)

BISHOP EZRA SARGUNAM

This article details the march of faith by the Evangelical Church of India towards the planting and shepherding of 1,000 churches among the responsive people groups and a membership target of 500,000 by 2000 AD. Eight hundred churches have already been planted.

The aggressive evangelism, discipleship and church-planting ministry by the ministers of the ECI with a holistic approach has already attracted world-wide attention.

Dr Billy Graham in his message felicitating me on my 50th birthday said, '... I hear wonderful reports of the ministry God has given you in India and the way he is richly blessing... May the Lord continue to bless you and use you in the time ahead until he comes ... Happy birthday.'

Dr Donald McGavran made the following observation about the ECI church-planting ministry:

The fascinating story of the unique church-planting ministry of ECI in India must be told everywhere in the pessimistic missionary world. What Dr Sargunam and his colleagues have achieved during the last two decades affirms that the Lord of the harvest is at work in several parts of India. I have been in a few of these churches and watched a number of baptisms. I commend Christians everywhere to support and claim a share in this tremendous victory, and help many more thousands to be discipled and churches multiplied until Christ returns.

Dr Ben Wati, the former General Secretary of the Evangelical Fellowship of India, had this to say about the ECI church-planting ministry:

There is no reason why this experiment cannot be multiplied all over India to see much church growth in this needy land.

Like Dr Ben Wati, there are hundreds of others who feel that the ECI model and experiment can very well be followed, and their efforts multiplied all over India or anywhere else in the world, wherever people are responding to the gospel of Jesus Christ.

IT ALL BEGAN IN PORUR, MADRAS

The ECI church-planting movement began in 1954. Though a few churches were already planted by that time, it was in a village called Porur near Madras that the first major break-through took place among the non-Christian community. I was posted here as an evangelist immediately after my biblical training in 1957. I rented a house for Rs 10/- a month and literally lived amongst rats and snakes. The Lord helped me to lead many young men to Christ through adult literacy classes.

One night, I was roused from my sleep by the clashing of cymbals and the sound of drums coming from a religious procession passing through the street in which I lived. It was Sivaratri (Shiva's night). Hundreds of men and women were going in a procession carrying their deity. Among the crowd I saw some of the young men who were attending my night classes. They were completely drunk and dancing before the deity. As I stood by the window, I literally broke down and kept saying to myself amidst sobs, 'What am I doing in this village?' I had thought that these men had become Christians, but their lives had not changed. Though their physical eyes were now open and they could read the Scripture and sing Christian songs, their inward eyes were not opened.

After this, I applied myself seriously to the task of discipling these men. Precisely a year later, on the same Sivaratri, the same procession was passing through my street. But on this night over 30 young men were there in my home taking part in an all-night prayer meeting. The break had come at last. These young men did not join the idolaters. All of them were baptized the same year in a Hindu temple tank as a witness to the community, and the Porur ECI Church continued to grow.

Today there are more than 600 believers in the Porur ECI Church, and almost 95% of them are first generation Christians.

It was here in Porur that God gave me the vision of the possibility of planting a church in every village and town. I had the affirmation that if the Lord could call thirty people out of a village, and there were hundreds of thousands of people out there, we could go and systematically evangelize every village and town. The vision caught on. So it all began in Porur, Madras.

What the ECI has experienced during the past forty years or so in discipling and multiplying churches among the responsive people groups has become a model for other evangelism and church-planting agencies. No other denomination which came into existence after Independence has grown so rapidly as the ECI. The Spirit of God has such an anointing on the ECI leadership's overall plan to disciple India's responsive population. I am not saying that we are the only ones out there. There are several other indigenous and overseas missions, which are planting numerous churches among various people groups.

For the encouragement and the benefit of church planters

around the world, I am giving here briefly some of the major factors behind our church's rapid growth.

THE MISSIOLOGICAL FACTORS BEHIND THE ECI CHURCH GROWTH

1. The Historic Background with OMS – A Church-Planting Mission

The most important factor in the ECI-OMS movement were its founders who were great men of faith and prayer, men of vision and mission with highly cherished principles. OMS International, the mother organization of ECI was founded in 1901 by Mr Charles E. Cowman and the senior Kilbourne with the definite call and vision to undertake extensive and intensive evangelism, planting of self-propagating, self-governing and self-supporting churches.

The ministry began first in Japan and then went on to Korea. OMS now operates in more than 14 countries with about 500 overseas missionaries and 5,000 national pastors, workers and evangelists. There are about 5,000 churches all over the world with a membership of about a million.

OMS entered India in 1941 and the first ECI Church was established in 1954. The church-planting ministry gained momentum only after 1974. ECI has now over 680 churches with a quarter of a million members. Basically, the ECI, and its founding organization the OMS, has always had a clear vision and objective, as to their strategy and modus operandi in training national leaders, equipping them in the ministry and sending them to responsive peoples to plant churches.

2. Fulfilling the Great Commission in toto

In the 'Go ... Preach ... Baptize ... Teach' Great Commission, our Lord has given us a package for evangelism and church-planting. Many send, some go, and a few preach but none go all the way out and baptize the followers, continuing to teach and shepherd them, gathering the new believers into groups of churches. Visionaries are many — missionaries are a few.

This is very much the secret of the success of the ECI ministry. Our workers do not confine their work to street-corner preaching, handing out a tract here and there or have relief and development projects just for the sake of it. They go all the way, not only in proclaiming the message but in following up the prospective enquirers to the extent that a new group of believers emerges and churches are planted. 'Preach, Persuade, Plant' is the slogan.

Obeying the Great Commission in its totality results in the birth and multiplication of churches. There is so much of seed sowing done these days throughout India, but there are very few who are willing to pay the price in watering the plants, nurturing them, weeding out the thorns and thistles that choke the plants, and harvesting the harvestable while they are ripe and ready to be harvested and gathering them into the barns.

3. Church-planting Seminary

Unlike the traditional seminaries which train 'parish priests for their denominations', the seminaries and Bible schools of ECI look beyond producing pastors for established churches. ECI does not depend on other Bible training institutes to train pastors for them. They train their own leaders. With a close-knit programme between the church and the seminary, the students are closely watched, disciplined and made to fit into the ECI mould. The students who do not like to be part of the ECI programme, leave sooner or later. Pioneer evangelism and church-planting is a painful process. Not many organizations are willing to choose this. They choose rather the easy and beaten path in the field of evangelism. The workers in the field and their supporters seem to be content with instant results, 'numbers' of decisions, hands raised, and heads down for reporting purposes. Though there is nothing wrong in this, any evangelism and discipleship programme that does not result in the nucleus of groups being formed and churches planted, may not have a lasting impact on the community it serves. Already 10 ECI Bible schools and seminaries are functioning, training evangelists, pastors and leaders for our church.

4. Focusing on the Responsive

ECI has specific policies and programmes to focus its evangelistic efforts among the responsive peoples of India. The oppressed and the suppressed are very responsive. ECI has multiplied churches by the hundred in the slums, among the scheduled castes and the scheduled tribes in the cities and villages. The people who are responsive today may not be responsive tomorrow. As in the ECI, an all-out effort must be made to disciple the most responsive.

5. Church Growth Through Transformed Lives

We have often heard pastors say 'My church is not growing, nobody comes to my church because I preach the truth, condemn sin or any appearance of evil.' But then, on the contrary, people could throng to your church because they find that Christianity works there and they find deliverance from their sins through heart-touching sermons in your church. This is how every local church should be. There was a man by the name of Munuswamy, owner of a laundry shop, who after a remarkable conversion led several people to Christ.

Balerao was once a bandit, operating in the Aurangabad area. There was a radical change in his life. He became a Christian and later an evangelist, revisited the villages he used to loot, but this time with the message of the gospel. Several hundreds accepted Jesus Christ, and 14 churches were planted. In January 1986, 3 mass baptisms took place in which 2,062 converts were baptized.

Arjun King, a witch doctor from Andhra Pradesh,

travelled all over India and under the influence of the evil spirit foretold the future of hundreds of people, including cinema stars and politicians. Once with his disciples, he even met Indira Gandhi and told her future. He earned a lot of money by soothsaying and the money ruined his life. He lived immorally and gave himself to drinking. Eventually, he lost his wealth and his health and came to the end of his resources.

Arjun King's sister became a Christian first and began witnessing to him. While he was camping in Madras in 1985, he happened to attend one of our Telugu churches. Pastor Pushparaj, the minister of this church, led him to Christ. I baptized him with the name Paul Arjun King along with the 13 members of his family. After becoming a Christian, he went to study in the ECI Bible School in Vijayawada. Even when he was a student he planted two churches. Paul Arjun King is an evangelist and a pastor and has a vision to disciple half a million people belonging to his community.

There are many such interesting stories in every village and town where ECI is involved in evangelism and church-planting. The message of the gospel becomes realistic and powerful when people see that it is operative in the lives of men and women.

6. Culture is Not a Barrier to Church Growth

ECI allows people to make a commitment and embrace the Christian faith without changing their social and cultural status, customs or traditions. Though casteism is not encouraged or promoted in the church, it is often seen that caste does not become a barrier to people becoming Christians. Wherever there are such pagan links with these cultures and customs, deculturization might become necessary. But this is done without creating a vacuum in the lives of the young converts. Under these circumstances, old traditions find new meanings after they are re-christened and brought into line with the Christian faith and practice. This deculturization process is known as 'functional substitute' in the study of missionary anthropology. The Hindu practices and rituals are replaced by Christian thanksgiving services.

It is the prime duty of the Christian evangelist to see that he does not upset the long cherished customs and traditions, but effects conversions with the minimum of social dislocations. This is religiously adhered to by the ECI in their ministry.

It may be observed that the cross in the centre of the ECI logo is deeply entrenched in the lotus, which is supposed to be the seat of the Indian gods. The inference is that the historical Christ and the cross must ultimately take the seat of these mythological deities and thereby Christianity should become deeply rooted in the culture of India.

7. Church Growth Through Power Encounter

Our Lord ordained the twelve not only to preach, but also to heal the sick and cast out demons (Mk. 3:14,15). Multitudes followed Jesus because of the signs and wonders he did. The early Christians added thousands everyday to the church through miraculous healings, followed by sound preaching of the gospel. The world is still looking today for signs and wonders. The moment people see the power of God demonstrated, they begin to make a commitment and are drawn closer to him.

Our Master said, 'Behold, I give you power (exousia) . . . over all the power (dunamis)' (Lk. 10:19). This should be our chief concern. We should demonstrate that power, as we confront people with the gospel of Jesus Christ.

People from every part of the world have their own problems and are looking for solutions to them. They go on a pilgrimage, take a 'holy' dip, climb mountains, walk on their knees, tonsure their heads, rend their bodies in an attempt to propitiate their gods and goddesses, trying to solve their problems and secure salvation from their sins and cure from their sicknesses. There are hundreds and thousands of people who are running from one guru to another, attending Christian divine healing campaigns for healing and deliverance. All our evangelistic efforts, our literature sales, door-to-door witnessing, street-corner preaching, film ministry, relief and development projects put together do not make any perceivable impact on the masses of India. Their problems remain the same.

When Christians go to the sick and express their love and concern for them and bring healing to them, they begin to put their trust in Christ. ECI places much importance on the practice of divine healing both within the body of Christ and among the non-Christians, where the ECI churches are located. Believers bring their ailing non-Christian neighbours to the church for healing. Couples who are without children are brought to the church and prayed for. In a number of cases the prayers have been answered. God touches the womb and children are born. There is a case of one Muni Naicker, a staunch Hindu from Dharmapuri (Tamil Nadu), in whose life God began to work when his sick cow was healed. Thereafter, he became a Christian and God gave him the gift of healing.

There were some other cases of healing and casting away of demons resulting in non-Christians turning to Christ in Nagrota, Kashmir, where Pastor Ratnam, himself a convert from a non-Christian faith, is ministering.

8. From Cities to Villages and Remote Tribal Areas

Missionary methods, whether St Paul's or ours, when they begin with cities and towns and then spread out to the surrounding smaller villages, do make a lasting impact. The shepherding of a congregation from cities to villages becomes relatively easier.

'By establishing the church in two or three centres, St Paul claimed that he had evangelized the whole province. Ten years after he started from Antioch, he told the Romans that he had fully preached the gospel of Christ from Jerusalem to Illyricum, and that he had no more place in which to preach in those parts. In this single sentence we have the explanation and the justification of St Paul's establishment of the churches in important centres. He had really and effectively occupied the province' (*Missionary Methods: St Paul's or Ours* (Allen), Page 19).

This strategy has worked well with ECI too. For example, in the city of Madras alone there are 106 churches. The message of the gospel has gone forth from the city of Madras to the neighbouring villages along the city-village lines. From Madras the fire has spread to Bombay, Goa, Delhi, Calcutta, Manipur, Gujarat, Orissa, Kerala and the Andaman Islands. People who move into the city are quite open to the gospel in the first few years, as they look for fellowship. When the gospel is presented to them, they are in a mood to listen and are also ready to make a commitment. When these young converts go back to their villages during vacations, they share their new faith with their friends and relatives. Before long, some of them are interested in the Christian faith.

This is how ECI has branched out from cities to towns and villages and has established contacts in remote areas and among the tribals when they move to cities looking for better prospects and job opportunities.

9. Church-planting in the City Slums

In Madras, Bombay and Calcutta, ECI has established a number of churches through day-care centres and relief and development projects – by ministering to the city slum-dwellers and taking care of their temporal needs.

The poor people who migrate from villages to cities, respond to the gospel more readily than the middle class or the elite.

10. The National Missionary Arm of the Church – the IMM

Every ECI believer is encouraged, challenged and motivated for direct involvement in the evangelization of India. The

Indian Missionary Movement was founded in the year 1974 for the sole purpose of serving as an indigenous mission agency for ECI. The IMM sends native missionaries, supported with funds raised mostly from ECI churches, to the areas where the seminary students or the ECC teams are not able to reach. At the moment there are 32 missionaries in Punjab, Orissa and Andhra Pradesh, who are fully or partially supported by IMM.

11. The ECI Partners

Another vital factor in the overall growth and development of ECI churches is the role played by some of the overseas and indigenous organizations. ECI was initially founded by OMS. Till now, OMS International continues to train leaders for the church through two of the seminaries in Allahabad and Madras as well as with the financial assistance towards the Every Creature Crusade Teams.

In the recent past, the vision of ECI and its overall church-planting capability and our holistic approach have been recognized by other evangelistic mission organizations like the Samaritan's Purse, New Directions Ministries, International Co-op Ministries, the Korea Evangelical Holiness Church and the Grace Community Church at Arizona, who have come forward to assist ECI with its programmes.

At the national level here in India, indigenous mission organizations like FMPB, Missionaries Upholders Trust, etc are planting churches for ECI, wherever feasible. The subsidy given by these funding agencies towards church building projects helps the ECI local churches to move much faster towards self-support.

CHAPTER 5

Revival in China –
The House-Church Movement

TONY LAMBERT

Director for Research,
China Ministries Dept, Overseas Missionary Fellowship

The elderly Chinese pastor beamed, as he ushered me to the front of his church in north-west China. 'You have come on the right day! We are having our baptismal service today', he told me. 'How many people are you baptizing?' I enquired. 'Oh, two hundred and fifty!' On another occasion I was visiting the huge church in the centre of Hohhot, capital of Inner Mongolia in the far north of China. Thousands of people were streaming out of the building after a service, as I tried to enter. Finally, when I made my way inside, I found the pastor. 'How many new converts joined your church in 1992?' I asked him. 'Eight hundred!' was the quick response. Again, in Shanghai, I met secretly with a house-church leader who had just returned from baptizing three hundred new converts in a remote rural region. In north China house-church leaders regularly baptize hundreds of new converts in underground streams, even during winter, when they have to break the ice.

These are just a few authentic examples of the massive church growth which China is experiencing today. Both officially registered and unregistered churches are seeing many new converts. Yet the large city churches, crowded to the seams, are just the tip of the ice-berg. Revival on an even greater scale is taking place in the vast rural hinterland of China, where many Christians meet informally in house-churches.

It is incredible today to realize that during the years 1966–1979 no churches were officially opened in China (apart from two 'show churches' for diplomats in Beijing). Between 1966 and 1976 the extreme Red Guards under the encouragement of Chairman Mao closed the last few remaining city churches, burned Bibles and sent pastors to labour camps. Christianity seemed to have been totally extinguished and a century of Protestant missionary endeavour to have been totally obliterated by atheistic communism. Overseas observers, including some Christians, were very pessimistic about the future of the Chinese church.

Yet today it is Maoism which is in deep crisis. The Chinese government pays lip-service to communism, but encourages rapid economic growth on increasingly capitalistic lines. A young teacher I met last year told me that his graduate students would laugh at him if he tried to teach history and politics from a Marxist viewpoint. Since the Beijing Massacre of June 1989 most educated young people have ceased to believe in Marxist theory, and many have turned to Christianity, packing the city churches, seeking answers. The collapse of Maoist ideology has created a great spiritual void and many Chinese people are seriously turning to religion. Protestant Christianity, in particular, has experienced a renaissance. Even the government admits that numbers of Protestants have risen from one million in 1979 to over seven million in 1994. The true figure is much higher, and a conservative estimate would be between 20–30 million, with some 10 million Roman Catholics.

The roots of the present revival must be traced back to

the dark days of persecution during the Cultural Revolution (1966–76), and even earlier when political pressures were increasingly placed on the Chinese church in the fifties. As the churches became more politicized, and dragooned under government control under the puppet organization known as the 'Three Self Patriotic Movement' (TSPM), many Bible-believing Christians quietly ceased to attend church and formed small Bible-study and prayer cells in the privacy of their own homes. Such meetings were prohibited and those discovered were liable to severe punishment. In 1966 all the churches were closed. Chinese believers today describe how they met clandestinely, sometimes holding copies of Mao's 'Little Red Book' in their hands to give the impression they were having a political study meeting, when, in fact, they were holding a prayer meeting. Preaching and singing were usually out of the question, as far too dangerous.

During this period the church of Jesus Christ was totally deinstitutionalized. Christians could no longer rely on their buildings, ceremonies, regular worship, pastors, preachers or even Bibles (most of which were collected and burnt by the Red Guards). True believers learnt how to rely totally on God and live for him while working in the militantly secularist and atheistic environment of Mao's China. Many suffered martyrdom or long imprisonment and their meekness and love made a strong impression on many. The reality of Christian love shone more brightly against the backdrop of 'class hatred' whipped up by Maoists. Christians memorized Scripture, and learnt to pray in secret. In the early seventies, following the Nixon visit to China, things eased very slightly, particularly in the coastal provinces where Christianity was strongest traditionally. Now larger house-churches were formed. People became more open in inviting neighbours and friends. One lady, a former Bible woman, opened a tea-shop for farmers in a remote mountain region. While the farmers talked and drank tea on market-days, she and a few believers held meetings in an 'upper room'. Gradually, more people were converted and a small church was formed. Similar things happened all across the country. Christianity was no longer a religious ritual reserved for Sundays, but had become a way of life – in most cases of the poor, the dispossessed, the peasants and the workers. The house-church movement in China thus resembled the spontaneous growth of the early church before Constantine, when believers met in the home, or beside the river, and church buildings were virtually unheard of.

The house-churches of China are intensely evangelical. Liberal theology withered away – it was no match for militant communism. Chinese house-church believers have a deep love for the word of God. For many years they were deprived of printed Bibles, and copies were painstakingly hand-written, often while listening clandestinely to gospel radio broadcasts from overseas. Although Bibles are now printed legally within China in limited quantity, there are still rural areas where, to my knowledge, one Bible has to be shared between more than one hundred believers. A hunger for God's word has developed which is scarcely understood in the opulent West. Chinese believers think nothing of standing in the rain or scorching sun to listen to preaching of the word of God for over an hour. Ten minute 'sermonettes' are unknown in China.

Chinese house-church Christians are men and women of prayer. Prayer meetings are marked by groans and tears and deep wrestling with God. It is the heartfelt conviction of Chinese Christians that the present revival has been the result of fervent prayer, and all the believers I meet always ask me to urge their brethren in the West to pray for them, not out of politeness, but because they know that God answers such prayer.

The Chinese house-church believers stress the new birth and the centrality of the atonement of Jesus Christ. In the West, the doctrine of the cross is in danger of being pushed aside by 'prosperity theology', 'liberation theology', 'feminist theology' etc. But in China, house-church evangelists carry the message of Jesus Christ and him crucified from village to village, travelling by bus, bicycle or on foot. The present revival has been born out of suffering. Many house-church leaders have been in prison for ten or even twenty years for refusing to compromise an inch with atheistic communism, or for refusing to join the compromised Three Self Patriotic Movement. They have a firm understanding that Christ is Lord of the church. In this, they stand in the spiritual succession to the heroes of faith down the centuries such as the Reformers, Covenanters and other martyrs who were prepared to lay down their lives for the sake of the gospel.

There is an energy and dynamism in Chinese house-churches. Worship is marked by reverence and awe, and sometimes by tears and fervent vocal prayer simultaneously. Chinese Christians have a strong expectation of God working in their midst in salvation and judgement. Sin is taken seriously. Those who compromise or fall away are admonished. Becoming a Christian is taken seriously as even today it can still mean discrimination – loss of one's job or a university place. Earlier this year in Beijing I met a top lawyer, a former member of the Communist Party, who openly renounced her party membership after becoming a Christian. She was instantly dismissed from her job, and for more than two years has been unemployed. Students and graduates who attend the officially registered churches, let alone the unregistered house-churches, may still be warned by Communist Party authorities to cease attending Christian worship. Pressures are usually more subtle than in the past, but still very real.

Chinese house-church Christians face real pressures. Even this year (1994) new restrictions have been introduced by the government at the highest level, enforcing registration of all Christian meetings. Many house-church people do not wish to comply for fear of suffering government and TSPM interference in their meetings, and restrictions on their evangelism. It is still illegal technically to witness to young people under the age of 18 in China and lead them to become church members. Sunday Schools are largely banned in the government-registered churches (with a few exceptions). The concern of the authorities to tighten control is proof of the success of the gospel.

Chinese house-churches are marked by a keen burden for evangelism. Those without Christ are regarded as lost and in need of salvation. Surrounded by Buddhist, Daoist and occult practices, particularly in the countryside, house-church evangelists seek genuine repentance and conversion and a clean break with past sin.

Let us now look at three specific examples of Chinese house-church evangelism, based on the reports of Chinese house-church leaders which I have translated. Pastor Lin Xiangao, better known in the West as Pastor Lamb, returned to Canton shortly after the Communist victory. In 1950 he began meetings in his home with 300 people attending. He was arrested in September 1955 and imprisoned by the communists for a year. He was re-arrested in May 1958 and held in prison for twenty years until 1978. He had memorized all the Epistles of Paul from Romans to Hebrews, by heart, and this stood him in good stead while in prison. For fifteen years he worked in the coal mines and linked up an estimated two million coal-carts. Others died or were badly injured, but God kept him alive. On his release in 1978 he returned to Canton and began to teach English, sharing the gospel with his students. In 1980 he held his first baptism of four new believers. Since then over 1,200 new believers have been baptized and his church at Damazhan has grown by leaps and bounds. He holds four services each week at which 300 people squeeze into his tiny home. In 1983 and again in 1988 and in 1990 he was severely interrogated by the government who put pressure on him to join the state-registered Three Self Patriotic Movement. In February 1990 sixty policemen stormed up the rickety stairs and hauled him off to be interrogated. They confiscated over 10,000 Bibles, hymn-books, tracts and Christian tapes and stripped the meeting-place bare of tape-recorders and amplifying equipment. He refused to register, and since his release has continued to hold meetings. Large numbers of educated young people, some of whom have good jobs

should be saved. It was the Holy Spirit who caused people to repent and believe and receive salvation. They only had to open their mouths to preach and without any effort on their part their hearers showed themselves willing to repent and believe. In a few days two brothers led 300 to believe in Jesus. Twenty others reported that more than 1,300 had been saved.

Some of the Christians went back two or three times to pastor the new converts. In Hubei a local witch, who had hindered many from believing, was converted. She, and many others turned to Christ. One team had no evangelistic experience, so they simply knelt down to pray fervently before preaching. On the first day 40 people were converted, and on the second, more than 200. While on a train, they led a university student to Christ, who publicly knelt down with them to pray.

This evangelism was not without cost. Most of the young people left well-paid jobs to live in very primitive conditions in remote rural areas. In a few cases they were forbidden to preach by the authorities and sent home. Some were fined. However, the churches of the entire region were stirred to practical evangelism to great effect.

By the end of April 1991 when most of them had returned they reported that more than 10,000 people had been saved!

Such a major evangelistic outreach is still unusual in China. In many areas the house-churches still have to be very low-key. However, with such zeal and vision it is hardly surprising that the church in China is growing rapidly. Already the evangelical community in China (if conservatively estimated at 20–30 million) is only second to that in the United States. If, as seems highly likely, the present rate of growth continues over the next decade or more, by the year 2,000 China will probably have the largest evangelical church of any country in the world. We in the West need to take note, and take to heart some spiritual lessons from this vibrant church which practises the preaching of the word of God and prayer, trusting in God and not in man's methods.

CHAPTER 6

Outside the Sanctuary: The Local Church and the Great Commission

DR TISSA WEERASINGHA

Senior Pastor, Calvary Churches, Sri Lanka

When it comes to sharing what we do in terms of evangelism and church planting, I am sure that all of us who are pastors can contribute points that can be helpful. The terrible mistake is to think that something that works in one place will automatically succeed in another. We know that is not so. Many times I have read of astounding growth and expansion somewhere and envied it for our church. Or I have looked at a very appealing programme in some other church and pondered whether it would work for me. Honestly, it may or may not. But, thank God we can learn from one another! That's the intent of this book. In this article I would like to share some of the factors that have worked for us. I hope it will inspire you.

1. MOBILIZING PEOPLE FOR EVANGELISM

One of the great challenges all of us pastors face is that we are constantly working with a volunteer force. This means that motivating them to be involved in kingdom work through the church can become a Herculean task. At the end of the day, if someone fails to do an assigned job, you cannot cut the pay! Motivating volunteers is quite different from motivating employees in a business. There are no tangible perks that we can guarantee down here.

But, people do get addicted to success. When they see results through their own ministries, that itself acts as a force within. So, how do we get to there from here? The key I believe, is in our approach to the gifts that God has given to all believers. Spiritual gifts enable people to serve effectively. This results in success which in turn breeds the desire for more of the same. The way we began to mobilize people was primarily through making people aware of what their gifts were. It appears that one of the commonest gifts in the church is the gift of exhortation (Rom. 12:8). Actually, this is a minor form of the gift of pastoring. I researched and found out all the different evidences of this gift, listed them all and ran a 'self-awareness test' at our training sessions. Most people who attended this, admitted that they qualified on the basis of the descriptions that had been itemised. Then they were mobilized as cell leaders and potential leaders. Continuous mobilization on the basis of the gift of exhortation ensures a constant supply of leaders for small groups and cells. Home cells have been our main strategy for evangelism and church planting.

2. USING CELLS FOR EVANGELISM AND CHURCH PLANTING

Home cells act as both an evangelistic and nurture mechanism and help us to locate responsive communities even when the general population may be characterized as resistant. The cell has a dual function when the meeting is so structured that it feeds the believers who come, as well as relating to the non-believers. One of the main ways we do this is by training the leaders in biblical exposition. Then they are shown how to present the latent evangelistic point, which I call the 'E' point in every expository message. [This system is described more fully in my book, '*Home Cell Manual*', Calvary Press, Sri Lanka]. Thus no one is left out and the cell always relates to new persons as well as old.

Whenever the composition of a cell is such that the number of unbelievers exceeds the number of believers, this is taken as a sign that we have penetrated a responsive community. We begin to strategize from then on for church planting. There are nearly 50 new churches that have been organized over the last 10 years since we began our church planting programme. All have been started through cells. When signs and wonders occur, it acts as a catalyst for church planting. In one remote village where the name of Christ had never been heard, a paralyzed man was miraculously healed. The word spread and some of the villagers got together and began to worship 'the God who is above' as they called him. This went on for a while and it so happened that one of our believers was transferred to that village. Our workers went in, told the people the name of the 'God who is above' and organized a new church. I wish this kind of thing would happen every day!

3. FINANCIAL STEWARDSHIP AND THE GREAT COMMISSION

Church growth and financial stewardship are quite closely related. People who give stay in the church they give to, because they are tied to it through their stewardship. The more serious matter is that in many countries in the Two-Thirds world, churches and pastors are heavily dependent on foreign aid and this creates apathy on the part of believers. On the other hand, when people are challenged to give even out of their 'affliction' like the Macedonian believers, their concern and burden for world evangelization increases. From day one of my pastoral tenure, our church began to raise local finances. It took us about 5 years to build our new building. But it was worth it. When the local believers support their pastors and workers, the prayer concern is much higher and there is concrete involvement in the fulfilment of the Great Commission. It is true that budgets have to be trimmed and programmes may have to be more critically examined. But this discipline is integral to growth. During a time of great hardship in the country, one of the ways we raised finances for our church was by asking people to give in cash or kind their most valuable things. What we raised one Sunday in this way was enough to give us a jump-start on our building programme. In many societies it is important to break the myth that the poor have no responsibility to give. The myth of the irresponsibility of the poor for the Great Commission has been the curse of missions development in the Two-Thirds world. We must teach people to give, not in order that they may get back from God, but because it is God's method for the saving of a lost world. He gave his best. We must teach our people to give sacrificially for the propagation of the gospel.

4. TRAINING LEADERS FOR CHURCH PLANTING

A strategy for church planting must also incorporate a method for raising adequate workers to cover the churches. Our method has been primarily to 'home grow' our leadership base. This applies even to our pastoral team. Therefore, we started a training institute in 1984. The institute does not admit everyone who wants training. We take only those who are currently engaged even at an initial stage in church planting. They must also be sure that they will devote their full time after graduation to Christian ministry. So they are screened well before they enter the school. During their training period of 2 years, they are practically engaged in planting a new congregation which they will take over on graduation. In this way, the dropout rate is minimal and the student builds his or her own base of ministry under close supervision. But church planting cannot be done alone. Therefore, there is on-going training of a lay ministry team together with this potential full-time worker. The main structure of training of lay persons is through the cells and practical experience in church planting. One of the important aspects of all training is the equipping of people in expository preaching techniques. Training sessions are conducted for this purpose. Some lay persons who have been trained in this manner have gone to foreign lands and as 'tent-making missionaries' have started churches there too. Very exciting reports are currently being received of the work of these missionaries in so-called closed countries.

5. TARGETED PRAYER

The impact of fasting and prayer to open up communities for church planting cannot be over-emphasized. In Sri Lanka, the belief in guardian deities, occultism, witchcraft and sorcery is rampant. We are well aware that whole communities are under demonic bondage and have been so for centuries. Satan does not release his strongholds easily. When we have made some inroads into a community, strategic prayer directed towards the spiritual and ideological intermediaries in that area results in a weakening of their power and ineffectiveness in their strongholds. In a new church in an area where there is some opposition to the work at the present time, the daughter of the village witchdoctor was miraculously delivered and healed after prayer. She had been incurably sick for several years. The witchdoctor, it appears, does not have too much power in his trade currently, and is also becoming positive towards the gospel. Continuous fasting and prayer by the leaders of this new church brought about this situation.

In one locality where a new church was planted among Hindus, when many came to Christ, the illicit brew business in that slum began to decline. The thugs who were running the business assaulted our believers and compelled the closure of the church. The believers were also forced to flee from the place. However, we continued to pray on target so that this church would be reopened. We believed that reopening it would really honour God. Not long afterwards, thugs from a neighbouring slum came over and murdered all the people who had assaulted our believers. The slum was 'cleansed' and our believers went back in and replanted the church. The majority of people there are now Christians and the work goes unhindered.

The link between prayer and the fulfilment of the Great Commission is never debated. But the way we pray is crucial. On occasion, it may be necessary even to pray imprecatorily. The psalmist did that often. Furthermore, we need to mobilize prayer at a national level. In March 1993, we felt compelled to challenge Christians in Sri Lanka to committed prayer for the nation. I asked people to pray for the nation every day for 5 minutes only. Today, the 'PRAYER FORCE', as we call it, has 4,700 partners from all churches and all parts of the country. We have an estimated 23,500 minutes of prayer going up every 24 hours for the nation! Many things have happened that cannot be detailed here. Suffice it to say that such prayer can only cleanse the atmosphere and facilitate the transmission of the gospel.

6. MINISTRY TO PERCEIVED NEEDS AS A STARTING POINT

Most people (except philosophers) do not spend their time thinking about ultimate realities. Their minds are occupied with things that are more mundane; their immediate realities and needs. Therefore in the propagation of the gospel, believers need to be taught how to minister to the perceived needs of people around them, and thereafter sensitize them to their need for salvation in Christ. Much of the training conducted in churches relates to how to function as the 'gathered community'. We train people in

Sunday school teaching, running youth meetings, functioning as elders and deacons and carrying out other activities related to our corporate life. This is very necessary. However, we may not be balancing this type of training sufficiently with another dimension. That dimension is, how the believers are to function as the 'scattered community'. This refers to how people minister outside the walls of the sanctuary. That is where they spend most of their time. Therefore, training programmes for evangelism need to be geared in that direction. Ministry to perceived needs acts as a hook to bring people to Christ. The relevance of this is heightened by our knowledge that most people in popular religious contexts come to Christ in two stages. The first stage is their realization of the helplessness of the 'gods' they have been worshipping. This often happens through ministry to perceived needs. The next realization is that they are sinners before God in need of repentance. The need for cleansing is something that emerges later. The sensitive evangelist will be aware of that. [I have dealt with this in greater detail in my book, *The Cross and the Bo Tree*, Asia Theological Association, Taiwan, 1989]. Otherwise the fruit will be plucked too early or not at all. Ministry to perceived needs is the factor that builds credibility and enables the communicator to get a hearing for the gospel. It opens doors. Therefore, more emphasis must be placed on the type of training that enables common, ordinary believers to be instruments of the Holy Spirit's power.

Finally, 'there is nothing new under the sun'. You may have recognized all of these things as the very factors that have helped you in your pastoral ministry. The issues I have enumerated in the preceding pages are those which helped us to reach people for Christ and plant churches in a context that is not very favourable to the gospel for so many historical and socio-religious reasons. But there is no limit to what God can do as we believe and expound his word and rely on the direction of the Spirit. Let his purpose for each church scattered all over the world be fulfilled.

CHAPTER 7

The Pastor and His Mission

DR S. J. SUTJIONO

Gereja Kristus Rahmani, Indonesia

By the grace of God and the work of the Holy Spirit, we began our church with 20 people in Djakarta, the capital city of the Republic of Indonesia, on December 12, 1971. From the Haggai Institute, founded by Dr John E Haggai, I learned how to set four goals for our church. These are:

1. A Loving Church (Jn. 13:34,35)
2. A Praying Church (Jam. 5:13–18)
3. A Witnessing Church (Ac. 1:8)
4. A Sending Church (Mt. 20:18–20; Mk. 16:15–18)

These goals are very important for the life of our church. The first goal is a loving church. If we confess that we are born-again Christians (Jn. 3:3,5) that means the Holy Spirit is in us and the fruit of the Holy Spirit is love (Gal. 5:22,23). The greatest commandment is to love the Lord and to love our neighbours (Mt. 22:37–40). We teach our church to love the Lord and the people in and outside the church who are still lost. This is a new command that we must love one another, there is no alternative. All people will see in this a testimony that we are disciples of Jesus

Christ. It is a bad testimony to this world if we fight with one another. Why? Because we aren't filled with the Holy Spirit, but by lust and evil spirits.

The second goal is 'a praying church'. As we know, there are many problems in our life and ministry, and we learn many methods to solve our problems. But prayer is the most effective and powerful way to solve our problems. Also, through prayer, God works mightily with wonders. One of our church members who was already dead was resurrected through prayer.

Prayer is God's tool and method. Why don't we become a praying people if we want to see God in action today? There are many problems and difficulties in both church life and Christian families, but God is faithful to help us in his right time (Ps. 37:1-7). Prayer changes things. The prayer of a righteous man is powerful and effective. Every morning we have a prayer meeting. We have a prayer chain, twenty-four hour prayer, all-night prayer and praying and fasting. Do you believe in the power of prayer?

The third goal is 'a witnessing church'. We teach our church members to become witnesses for Christ as their target in life. Before they are baptized, they have to attend baptism classes every week for between three and six months where they are taught the assurance of salvation, five principles to promote growth in faith, the trinity, the church, witnessing, giving, etc. They are questioned before they are baptized on the assurance and evidences of their salvation, prayer life, devotion time, church attendance, and on winning souls for Christ, etc. These are the basic requirements for baptism. A few of the questions asked are:

Do you have assurance of your salvation?
Are you sure that you will go to heaven?
Can you bring anything to heaven?

Their response would be that they believe that they can take only souls to heaven. Souls are precious to the Lord; he came and died on the cross, and this awareness should mobilize all members of the church to be his witnesses –

to lead people to himself. The result of this is that each year hundreds are baptized in our church.

The last goal is 'a sending church'. The heart of God is mission. The church is blessed if she becomes a mission church. We learn and work to fulfil the Great Commission to send people, or to give money to build churches on other islands or in other places. So we build churches in the whole of Java, Sumatra, Kalimantan, and Hong Kong.

1. PASTOR'S VISION
(Matthew 9:35–38)

There are three visions for pastors:

a) Geographical Vision

'Jesus went through all the towns and villages, teaching in their synagogues, preaching the good news of the kingdom and healing every disease and sickness' (v.35). We don't work only in the cities, but also in the villages. We have to teach and train the church to have vision and mission, and to preach the good news, to reach out and win souls.

b) People-oriented Vision

'When he saw the crowds, he had compassion for them, because they were harassed and helpless, like sheep without a shepherd' (v.36). Do you have compassion toward people, especially the lost? They live in darkness without hope, are going to hell, are harassed and helpless like sheep without a shepherd. Do you love them? This vision moves us to love and have compassion toward all people who are lost.

c) Evangelistic Vision

Jesus said to his disciples: 'The harvest is plentiful but the workers are few. Ask the lord of the harvest, therefore, to send out workers into his harvest field' (vv.37,38). Can we see that the harvest around the world is plentiful?

I pray day and night for the Lord to work through all his servants and children, through churches and para-churches, and to anoint and use them. The Holy Spirit works in evangelism through radios, films, cassettes, books, revival meetings, etc. Today, thousands of people will come and believe in the Lord Jesus Christ. So I work hard through teaching, preaching, conducting seminars, writing books and papers. Jesus is coming soon. How do we redeem our time which is so short?

' "My food", said Jesus, "is to do the will of him who sent me and to finish his work. Do you not say, 'Four months more and then the harvest'? I tell you, open your eyes and look at the fields! They are ripe for harvest" ' (Jn. 4:34–35). My vision is that the coming of our Lord is soon. (Rev. 22:12,20). The time is short, so we ought to redeem the time. The night will come when we cannot work. While we still have time, we must work hard.

At present, my ministries are pastoring the church which has two thousand members, teaching at seven departments in the Indonesian University and Academy, and writing more than forty books. On August 31, 1992 we started a Cross-Cultural Theological Seminary and I am teaching there also. My vision is that through this seminary we can send thousands of missionaries around the world. I also teach at the Institute of Church Growth and help other seminaries and churches in training. I help in advising revival meetings in Djakarta: for example the Luis Palau Evangelistic Association gave me 'The Co-Laborer Award' and the Haggai Institute gave me the Silver Anniversary Award for Outstanding Christian Service.

2. PASTOR AS A PROBLEM SOLVER
(Acts 6: 1–7)

The church often has many problems because we deal with people and face the devil. There are five principles in dealing with problems:

a) A pastor should be a man who is filled with the Holy Spirit

How can we be filled with the Holy Spirit? Firstly, we have to confess and repent of our sins (1 Jn. 1:9) and ask that the blood of Jesus purify us from all sins (1 Jn. 1:7; Isa. 1:18). Secondly, we offer our bodies as living sacrifices (Rom. 12:1). We surrender to God totally. Thirdly, we ask to be filled with the Holy Spirit (Lk. 11:11–13). Lastly, we believe that we are already filled with the Holy Spirit and the fruit of the Holy Spirit is love, joy, peace, patience, kindness, goodness, faithfulness, gentleness, and self-control (Gal. 5:22,23). So the Holy Spirit helps us in our weaknesses (Rom. 8:26) to control our mind and heart. The Holy Spirit helps us to solve problems.

b) A pastor should be a man of wisdom

If we lack wisdom, we ask God who gives it generously (Jam. 1:5). The fear of the Lord is the beginning of knowledge (Prov. 1:7). 'Therefore everyone who hears these words of mine and puts them into practice is like a wise man' (Mt. 7:24,25). We need wisdom like Solomon to solve the problems; we need to ask wisdom from God and to practise his words in our daily life.

c) A pastor should be a man of prayer

We learn many methods to solve our problems but there is one method that God gives us to use and that is prayer. It is very powerful and effective. The prayer of a righteous man is the prayer offered in faith (Jas. 5:13–18). Why don't you pray to solve your problems? He will show his power, his mercy, and his love to you. He, the living God, will answer your prayer. He changes things. (Ps. 37:5–7).

d) A pastor should be a man of his word

His word cleans our life (Jn. 15:3). His word is a lamp and a light to our life (Ps. 119:105). If we have current problems or troubles which can mean we live in darkness, only God's word can give us light to solve our problems. If we delight and meditate on his word, whatever we do prospers (Ps. 1:2,3). His word and his promises become our strength and comfort in troubles.

e) A pastor should be a man of faith

We have hope when we put our faith in Christ. 'And hope does not disappoint us, because God has poured out his love into our hearts by the Holy Spirit, whom he has given us' (Rom. 5:5). We believe that 'nothing is impossible with God' (Lk. 1:37).

Jesus Christ is the same yesterday and today and forever (Heb. 13:8). God has said, 'I will never leave you, I will never forsake you.' So we say with confidence, 'The Lord is my helper, I will not be afraid.' (Heb. 13:5,6). We ought to commit our problems to the Lord, trust in him and he will help us to solve our problems. (Ps. 37:5–7). Do you have faith?

3. PASTOR'S LEADERSHIP

a) The concept of Peter Wagner's 'Servant-Leader' can be added to the 'fatherly approach' in the Indonesian leadership context. As the chairman of our church synod, I use this fatherly approach in dealing with many cases or crises in our churches, with conflict among pastors, elders, deacons and church members.
b) Multiple leadership is very important in the life of the church. So I train our church members (laymen) to be leaders. There are many churches (about 50 daughter churches) that have been established by our lay-pastors in Djakarta. If we want our church to grow, we ought to teach our church members to win souls, and to train them to become church planters and leaders. Rome was won by laymen.

c) The pastor's leadership is an influence, inspiration and encouragement for our church members and leaders outside our organization.

4. PASTOR'S EXAMPLE
(2 Timothy 4:11,12)

Sometimes the pastor has a childish and self-pitying attitude. But we should be mature in faith and spiritual life. There are five principles for growth in spiritual life: the word of God, prayer, fellowship, sharing, and obedience to God.

There is a close relationship between teaching and living. Speaking and doing deeds are one. Deeds speak louder than preaching. We must set an example for believers. The areas that need to be exemplified are:

a) In Speech

We should understand the value of speech, because as preachers, we spend most of our time speaking in the pulpit, and as counsellors, we give direction and advice. Overall, as leaders, we also have to keep promises for any appointments. How can we became examples if we fail in our speech? Can we be trusted in what we say?

b) In Life

Our way of life, our attitude in life, and our spiritual life are important areas to be taken care of. The centre part of our life is our heart. Does the Holy Spirit rule our hearts and minds? Is Jesus Christ the Lord in our life? There is only one life that will be blessed – the life for Christ and his kingdom – and that is a fruitful life. As Paul has said, 'For to me live is Christ and to die is gain. If I am to go on living in the body, this will mean fruitful labour for me . . .' (Phil. 1:21,22).

c) In Love

All believers in our church will see the pastor's love. Love begins with our family, then our congregation, then to the lost souls outside the church. This love is a reflection of that of our Lord Jesus Christ.

We should be sensitive to the needs of people and always want to help them. Sometimes we visit our church members who are poor and sick, and we see that they don't need only visitation and prayer, but also need money to go to the doctor and to pay for medicine and food. Love means that we are willing to sacrifice something. Love means that we are concerned for the needs of people. Love means giving ourselves and what we have.

d) In Faith

Sometimes we exhort other people to have faith, but we don't have faith ourselves. The people know when we have faith or not. For example, in financial matters of church buildings and programmes, do we believe that God will provide for our needs? If we work according to his will and to his plan, for his glory and kingdom, we believe that God will work through us and in us. Jesus said, 'I tell you the truth, anyone who has faith in me will do what I have been doing. He will do even greater things than these' (Jn. 14:12–14).

e) In Purity

Today is a day of darkness. There is pollution in the minds and hearts of people. There is lust of the flesh, lust for money and position and rule over people. There is 'sexual immorality, impurity and debauchery, idolatry and witch-craft, hatred, discord, jealousy, fits of rage, selfish ambition, dissensions, factions and envy, drunkenness, orgies and the like' (Gal. 5:19–21). One day, a Christian shared his testimony and asked someone to believe in Jesus Christ, but he answered, 'I don't believe in Jesus Christ, because the pastor has taken my wife!' How can a Christian give a good testimony if he lives a wicked life? But 'blessed are the pure in heart, for they shall see God' (Mt. 5:8).

5. PASTOR'S FAMILY

The pastor's family is like 'a city on a hill which cannot be hidden' (Mt. 5:14). All people, and especially our church members, will see us. Our family is like a glass house – where people can see what is going on inside, so we cannot be hidden.

Often we seek the lost sheep outside, but our own children in our home are lost. The pastor's family is very important. My mother wanted me to marry Betsy, but I wondered whether she was fit for a pastor's wife. So I prayed, 'Lord, I want to be your servant. If it is your will that I marry Betsy, please give me a sign!' And the Lord answered my prayer. Professor Dr J. L. Ch. Abineno, former president of the National Council of Churches of Indonesia, and also my best friend, said to me, 'You are blessed because of Betsy.' Dr Han Chul Ha, President of ACTS and a group of leaders from South Korea unexpectedly came to our home at lunchtime. So, I asked Betsy, without any notice, to prepare lunch for our honoured guests. After lunch, Dr Han said, 'She is truly a pastor's wife.'

We have three children – two daughters and one son. I have heard it said many times that the worst children are the children of pastors. I found that there are three reasons for this. Firstly, the devil attacks the pastor's family constantly. Secondly, as a result of the business of the pastor and his wife in ministry, they hardly have any time with their children. Thirdly, they live in pastoral houses which are located beside or at the back of the church. There is the danger that if the church members love their pastor too much, they want to give many things to the pastor's children, but this is not good for the children's education. However, if the church members don't like their pastor, it affects their children also. The ideal is that the pastor's family should live apart from the church, but the raising of funds to rent or buy a house for the pastor's family can be a problem.

To solve these problems, we should have a family devotion time where we pray together. Here we teach our children how to pray, and through this they will know Christ better. We pray for God's protection so that we don't fall into temptation, but God delivers us from the evil one and puts the hedge around us (Job 1:10). We have to make time for the children – for fellowship, to give direction, to teach and give them examples through our lives as parents like Monica, the mother of Augustine.

I heard a testimony from Dr Ramesh Richard, the son of Dr D. John Richard, who is a professor at Dallas Theological Seminary, who said that he has the best father and is proud of him. He is a life example for his son in deeds and faith.

We thank God for our children. Maritha, our eldest daughter, graduated from university and married Agus, the Head Administrator of Staffing at the church. Samuel, the second child, graduated from Texas State University; he is currently working as a manager of the Bank in North Carolina and assisting his pastor in foreign students' ministry. Rohana, our youngest daughter, graduated with a Masters from Columbia Biblical Seminary (Columbia International University). She is helping me in local church ministry and gives lectures at the Cross-Cultural Theological Seminary. Children are the fruits of grace of God for his glory and his kingdom.

6. PASTOR'S MISSION

The pastor's mission is not only in the local church but also the whole world. The local church is the pastor's base to launch the work for the whole world. Our local church should be a mission church – to pray, support people financially, and send people to other parts of the world.

How can a church become a mission church?

a) We give vision to the whole congregation, so we have one vision.
b) We set goals for our church. The whole congregation should agree with the goals of the church.
c) We should pray together, share and work together as a united church (Phil. 2:1–5).

Through our local churches, we opened five Christian schools from kindergarten up to senior high school where we have thousands of students. In Djakarta, we also have the Doulos Training Centre and Cross-Cultural Theological Seminary. In Surabaya, the second largest city in Indonesia, we have a Mission School to train young people for village work. Our church is working together with ETSI (Evangelical Theological Seminary of Indonesia) – which was founded by Dr Chris Marantika for church planting – on a programme called 1:1:1. In one generation, we plant one church in one village.

We started our church with twenty people, now there are more than 150 churches that consist of fifteen thousand church members in different parts of Indonesia and in Hong Kong. Also through a local church, we have opened a small clinic. Our church sends me to help other churches in Indonesia and abroad. The role of the pastor in mission is vital and important. As pastors, we should expand our vision and ministry. The whole world is our parish, not only our local church. This should be our mission for his glory and kingdom.

CHAPTER 8

The Vision, Strategy and Priority of Truth Lutheran Church (Taipei, Taiwan) For the Year 2000

REVD PETER N. Y. YANG

In the past few years, more and more brothers and sisters are beginning to be concerned about the vision and strategy of Truth Lutheran Church. I do agree that we should have vision and strategy for the ministry of the church, but what is more important is how we can get our vision and strategy. Two years ago, there was a special opportunity for me to have a conversation with Revd Taylor, former president of the China Evangelical Seminary. I asked him to give me some words of encouragement and blessing when the conversation came to an end. What he said was very precious and unforgettable to me! The key was to know more about the Lord. He said that if he had known our Lord, our God more, there would have been a greater difference in his ministry.

Our vision and strategy should come from our knowledge of the Lord. If you look at the biblical history of salvation over two thousand years of church history, any individual or group of people that has been used by the

Lord are those who have met him and known him before they fulfilled their ministry. When Joshua was leading the Israelites into the promised land of Canaan, he needed to know who the captain of the host of the Lord was (Josh. 5:13–15).

Forty years have passed for Truth Lutheran Church. In Chinese thinking, the fortieth year is the year of certainty. We cannot be certain, have vision, strategy or priority unless we know our Lord. Facing the year 2000, the vision, strategy and priority of Truth Lutheran Church is based completely on the knowledge of our loving Lord Jesus Christ and his work of salvation on the cross (1 Cor. 2:2). This is also the foundation of all the ministry in this church.

When we think of our Lord Jesus and him crucified, we should know two things. Firstly, from the cross of our Lord Jesus, we know that our God is an omnipotent and merciful God. Secondly, from the love of the cross we are encouraged to walk gladly the way of the cross. The source of our enthusiasm for the ministry comes from our understanding of the love of the Lord.

Starting from 'Jesus and him crucified' we will do our best to equip all saints, to establish a full Cell Group Church, to reach the unreached, and to plant more churches.

STATEMENT OF THE VISION, STRATEGY AND PRIORITY OF TRUTH LUTHERAN CHURCH FOR THE YEAR 2000

Foundation

1 Corinthians 2:2 'For I resolved to know nothing while I was with you except Jesus Christ and him crucified.'

Vision

Facing the coming of the year 2000, Truth Lutheran Church will continue to base all its ministry on the Theology of the Cross (1 Cor. 2:2). We are determined to accomplish the following three commissions by the grace of our Lord Jesus Christ.

1. To reach the goal of shepherding, namely, to equip all saints (Eph. 4:11–13) and establish Truth Church to become a full Cell Group church filled with the Holy Spirit and fulfil the following functions within the cell groups:
   a. worship and prayer
   b. fellowship of love
   c. outreach and compassionate service
   d. discipleship training
2. To establish fifty to one hundred Cell Group churches in Taiwan. (Each with 100–200 members)
3. To meet the needs of worker training of world-wide Chinese churches.

Strategy

i) Sunday Service

To develop an exciting and meaningful worship celebration every Sunday through music and the pulpit ministry.

ii) Prayer

a. We should pray that all members may clearly experience being born again and filled with the Holy Spirit.
b. Each member should participate in fasting and prayer each week in anticipation of the second coming of Jesus Christ.
c. Teams of intercessors should pray daily for the church and church leaders.

iii) Cell Groups

a. Cell groups are outreach-oriented. Growth and division is expected after 6 months.
b. Cell group leaders see prayer and individual discipleship as their first priority.

c. Worship and praise, Bible study, serving and intercession, and sharing of the vision of outreach are goals for all cell group members, to help believers to develop a life-style under the cross.
d. Members should be helped to establish wholesome Christ-like families (at least 100 fully devoted families of prayer and gospel sharing will be established) and to maintain a correct Christian view of their vocations. Both their families and the following of their vocations should witness strongly to the Lord.

iv) Outreach and Service

a. Evangelism within the church – special conferences, cell groups, and individual evangelism as channels to bring out compassionate service.
b. Evangelism within the island – church planting in the vicinity of universities and colleges.
c. Evangelism outside of the island – co-working with overseas Chinese churches for church planting; university-centred cities will be our first priority.

v) Discipleship and Leadership Training

a. Within the church – there will be theology courses and disciple training courses for all church members. This will include strengthening service to the children and youth education. All possible ways will be used to produce effectively cell group leaders.
b. Within the island – we will co-operate with other churches on the island to help them with leadership training.
c. Outside of the island – we will co-operate with overseas Chinese churches to help them with leadership training.

vi) Relationship of co-workers

a. There will be recruitment of full-time workers for shepherding and church administration for the part-time workers to reduce unnecessary pressure from meetings and co-ordination and focus on outreach ministry. Better co-operation between the full-time and part-time workers will be promoted to improve the efficiency of church work.

b. Improving the relationship among church workers both from churches within the island and abroad.

vii) Facilities and Apparatus (Hardware)

Multi-functional and multi-purpose facilities are considered first to meet the needs of shepherding, evangelism and compassionate service.

Priority

People – Software (Programme) – Hardware (Facilities)

1. Dedicate oneself to the Lord and the body of Christ.
2. Dedicate oneself to the society (family and vocations).

CHAPTER 9

Evangelism Through Counselling

PASTOR NABUO TANAKA
Kojo Church, Japan

We feel privileged to share about how God has blessed us here at Kojo Church in Yonezawa city, Japan, and how our church is helping to advance Christ's Kingdom in Japan and overseas.

I. OUR ROOTS

Let us first give you a picture of the background of our 600–member church. Revd Nabuo Tanaka's father, Yoshio, was baptized by Revd Kagawa during the Holiness Revival in Tokyo in the 1950s. After a brief training period he was out in street evangelism almost every day. The rationing just after World War II was tight, and as a result, his sacrificing wife gave much of her food to little Nabuo, and eventually she died of starvation. When our present pastor Nabuo sometimes speaks of Calvary love and how his mother gave her life for him, there is not a dry eye in the audience. Pastor Yoshio Tanaka, in grief after losing his wife, took three-year-old Nabuo north to Yonezawa city to start a new life as an evangelist in a small holiness church. He remarried and was soon out again on the streets of this conservative Buddhist city of 90,000 people, beating the gospel drum, marching through town and holding evangelistic meetings in the revival days of the 1950s. This was when the flood of over 1500 American missionaries spread out all over Japan after World War II. Nabuo can remember those tough days as a boy in very meagre quarters. He would sell vegetables from door to door to help the family budget. He was developing leadership qualities in his school days, and inherited the witty humour of his father, as well as the spiritual warmth of his second mother, Kiyono-sensei. After a rebellious time, when Nabuo vowed to himself that he would never become a pastor, he recommitted himself to serve God, and entered a Christian University in Tokyo. By 1967, his dream of studying in the USA came true. He enrolled in Asbury Seminary in Kentucky, studied hard, and eventually completed his MA in psychology. He married a lovely Japanese-American lady called Jane. God called them back to Japan to help in the small church in Yonezawa where his father Yoshio had gathered about 20 believers. It was quite a shock for Nabuo's elegant wife Jane to move into the draughty old church in the Yonezawa snowdrifts in 1976. She was emotionally drained and on the verge of collapse, but God's encouragement and Nabuo's positive faith brought her through to become a strong woman of prayer and a notable leader for the Christian workers who would soon be working with them.

Nabuo had been influenced by Robert Coleman and others just after the glorious revival at Asbury, so he was fired up to win and disciple some young people for Jesus in his hometown. He used his ability in the English language at first to start English classes at the church, and gained many friends. One by one they gave their hearts to Jesus. During the first ten years there, about ten souls each year were led to faith and baptism. Close to one million dollars was raised to pay for the beautiful sanctuary, built in 1982 to hold 160 people there in the centre of

Yonezawa city. This Kojo Church became a centre of activity, not just on Sunday, but every day of the week.

II. HELPING HURTING PEOPLE

Pastor Nabuo has a wonderful way of attracting new workers, and seeing the possibilities in each person he meets. He knew well that many of those coming to church in Japan would be those with psychological problems and a sense of insecurity. His positive gospel of forgiveness in Jesus was just what they needed. Calvary grace was his central theme, as he preached through various books of the Bible.

The counselling ministries in the church flourished as Nabuo and his staff touched many people, and God brought inner healing. Jane often laid hands on them and ministered physical healing also, in the name of Jesus. Before long Nabuo knew he must train more Christian counsellors or else he would be completely swamped with people wanting attention. So the 'Total Counselling School' was officially launched in 1986, with Mrs Yuko Watanabe eventually taking charge of the nation-wide series of counsellor-training seminars. Nabuo had compassion for the many Christians throughout Japan who were indeed saved, but were still hurting because of unresolved inner conflicts, complexes and fears. He now conducts counsellor-training seminars in 12 cities throughout Japan. Currently, during one year, about 2,000 Christians and non-Christians are enrolled for these seminars on four levels, learning to accept themselves and finding emotional healing.

At first many ladies would apply for 'studying counselling', but actually they were hungry to find solutions for their own hurts and family problems. Nabuo aimed to begin new churches in various cities through these counselling class contacts who started seeking the Lord. So far, four such churches have been started, and 20 other home video-meetings are already functioning. Pastor

Nobuo and Jane believe that all things are possible by Christ's power!

Alcoholics have been converted. Lesbians, schizophrenic people, co-dependent persons, school drop-outs, people with eating or sleeping disorders, and those afflicted by demons have been set free and healed. Recently Jesus opened several deaf ears at healing meetings held by New Zealander Malcolm McIllwaith. One school drop-out named Mr Kinto has been converted and restored, led through to scholastic honours in college, and is now studying to be a pastor. A depressed school teacher named Mr Nagamine, who almost succeeded in killing himself by exploding a gas bomb, has been gloriously converted and is now a flourishing gospel singer in our church. When the people at his concerts around the country see his scarred face and hands and then hear him sing about how God transformed his life from fear to faith, they are often moved to tears. Several former Unification Church members have been brought to our church by their desperate parents for de-programming. Six of these precious young people have been delivered from the Moonie deception and are now gladly serving the Lord Jesus in our church.

Whoever comes, we try to accept them just as they are, loving them to Jesus, building up their confidence so that they will be able to decide for Christ and for baptism, in spite of opposition from the family. The community of love among our staff contributes much to the healing of these hurting people who come to stay with our staff in their homes and dormitories. We believe that Jesus, by his Holy Spirit, can make something good out of even the worst situations. This is our 'one-dimension' concept of grace – God 'works all things together for good to those who love him' (Rom. 8:28).

III. STAFF TRAINING

At present we have about 30 full-time staff. They are mostly volunteers. They include 10 pastors and evangelists, 4 counsellors, 10 seminary students, and 5 other office workers. About 10 additional staff help part-time in tape-packaging, telephone counselling, clerical work, and evangelism. Many of these workers are still in the process of regaining confidence after years of struggle with inferiority complexes, so they can sympathize well with hurting people. A warm atmosphere fosters healing, and Pastor Nabuo Tanaka's morning 'training talks' always challenge the staff to face their faults honestly, to receive forgiveness from God, and to try hard to strengthen their characters and reach out in evangelism.

About 10 of our staff are officially enrolled in our ACTS seminary programme (Agape Christian Training School). Nathan Mikaelsen has been in charge of ACTS since it was founded in 1990, training these future leaders. Six of our pastors teach a wide range of Bible subjects in the three-year curriculum. A rigorous schedule of practical church work is coupled with academic learning. Some graduates remain at the home church and others are sent out to other places. Revd Tanaka also teaches counselling classes at JTJ, the largest Protestant seminary in Japan, located in Tokyo.

IV. BOOKS, TAPES, VIDEO CHURCHES, AND LECTURE EVANGELISM

Since 1988, God has led us to develop a network of home groups around Japan. We now have 28 video churches called 'Gospel Houses' in cities scattered all over Japan. Typically, the believers worship together in the leader's home, inviting friends to watch Revd Tanaka's video message. Then they pray together, sing praises to the Lord, and counsel those with pressing problems. These Gospel Houses range in size from 44 people to 3 or 4. The first 'model' group was formed in Sendai city at Dr Ogasawara's home in 1987.

The attractive positive messages of Revd Tanaka have spread like wildfire all over Japan in the form of tapes, videos, and now over 20 books that are best-sellers on the Christian market here. 60,000 tapes are distributed each year, and 10 video tapes are also on sale presenting messages on positive thinking, deliverance from emotional sickness, 'How to help school dropouts', and 'The How-tos of Gospel Magic'. Pastor Tanaka often gives inspiring and humorous messages at schools, companies, banks, and church gatherings. He also speaks at Gospel Concerts with audiences of over 800 people, held in several cities each year.

V. WORLD MISSION OUTREACH

Our first overseas mission has been through the tapes of Pastor Tanaka which are sent to Japanese people overseas in Taiwan, the Philippines, Brazil, the USA, Canada, and Austria.

Now in 1995, we have opened a new Missions Centre in Sendai city in co-operation with our sister church, Gateway Centre in Brisbane, Australia. In Sendai, the Mikaelsens and Midgleys plan to train and commission 20 missionaries for overseas evangelism and church planting by 2000 AD. Our cell-group-type church raised up in Sendai will form a solid base of financial and prayer support for these missionaries, who will minister the gospel primarily to unreached people groups. Spiritual warfare and intercession ministry will play a large role in kingdom expansion.

Our Kojo Church is trusting God for the strength and wisdom needed to win thousands of Japanese people for Christ in Japan as well as many multitudes of souls overseas. Please pray for us so that we can keep humble before the Lord, always be on fire for him, and follow his directions in every way.

TO GOD BE THE GLORY!

CHAPTER 10

A Cell Church is Not a Church with Cells

LAWRENCE KHONG

Senior Pastor, Faith Community Baptist Church, Singapore

In 1986, God released me from another pulpit and challenged me to launch a cell church in Singapore. Previous experience had convinced me that this church would have to abandon traditional church structures. I had concluded that using small groups for fellowship, Bible study and prayer was not a New Testament pattern. Thus, we launched Faith Community Baptist Church as a fresh planting, without any commitment to use traditional programmes which would hinder our objective of winning the unreached for Christ.

By 1988, God gave us 54 cell groups. We developed a three-part vision which has guided our strategy ever since:

(1) To establish integrated ministries of outreach, discipleship and service which encompass the whole of Singapore.
(2) To be a church that provides a quality pastoral internship to pastoral candidates from all over the world.

(3) To establish 50 cell group churches around the world by 2000 AD, sending out teams to reach hidden or responsive people groups.

In order to achieve this vision, we built our structure using these biblical principles:

(1) Every believer is a minister, and must be equipped for service. The church of Christ is to become a spiritual army with Christians trained to set Satan's captives free.

(2) Believers should be organized into cell groups, similar to military squads. Each cell would be trained to edify one another and to evangelize so that it will multiply in less than a year, with a maximum size of 12–15 persons.

(3) Cell groups would not be considered 'house churches' but basic Christian communities linked together to penetrate every area of our community.

(4) Approximately five cell groups cluster to form a subzone, with a volunteer zone supervisor to pastor the five cells and its cell leaders.

(5) Five subzones cluster to create a zone of about 250 people pastored by a full-time zone pastor.

(6) Four or five zones cluster to form a district, with a seasoned pastor to shepherd approximately 1,000–1,250 people.

(7) As the senior pastor, I set out to develop a leadership team to assist me in providing maximum assistance to those involved at each level of ministry.

From the start, we created zones that were geographical (north, east, west) and generational (children, youth, college, career, military). Later, we added our music zone for those participating in our choirs, bands, orchestras, drama, and dance. We have rejoiced to discover that in 1993 the music zone produced the largest number of conversions per capita.

Soon after we formed the church, Dr Ralph Neighbour joined us to provide guidance as we began to shape the cell church structure. Working together, we created the foundations for our ministry. Pastors who had no previous experience with cell church structures were trained and cell leaders were equipped. Non-existent equipping materials had to be written. Soon we had a nickname: 'Fast Changing Baptist Church'! With every experimental step, we learned how to equip and evangelize in the new paradigm. With a determination to discard anything that did not help us achieve our goals, we revised our strategy over and over again as we gained experience. Indeed, we are still doing so!

Like other cell churches, our life involves three levels: the cells, the congregations (a cluster of five cells), and the celebrations on Sunday. We quickly had to go to two and then three celebrations of 1,000 people to accommodate the growth in the cell groups. We presently have four major services each Sunday of two hours duration. We have studiously avoided advertising 'seeker-sensitive services' choosing instead to grow through the ministries of our members in the cells. For us, the celebration is an assembling of the body of Christ rather than a means of attracting the unconverted. In spite of this, we have recorded hundreds of conversions every year as a result of the evangelism of our cell groups.

A major spiritual breakthrough came for us in those early years as we began to recognize the place of the gifts of the Holy Spirit in our midst. As cell groups confronted by the need for spiritual power in caring for people, we saw a gracious outpouring of his presence in our midst. We shall never forget a Sunday when God came with such power that the entire auditorium was filled with people overwhelmed by his presence. Our cell groups learned to minister in the power of the Spirit.

'The Year of Equipping' has become an important part of our cell group life. Each incoming member is visited by the cell leader, who assigns a cell member to be a sponsor for the new person. A 'Journey Guide' is used to acquaint the cell leader and sponsor with the spiritual condition of the person. Guided by private weekly sessions with the sponsor, this person will complete a journey through the

'Arrival Kit' and then be trained to share Christ with both responsive and unresponsive unbelievers. In addition, each member's journey includes a one-year survey of the entire Bible using 'Cover the Bible' and audio tapes which give me five minutes a day to teach our members about the Scriptures.

Because of our strong desire to penetrate the society around us, we formed the Touch Community Services. Through this separate corporation, we conduct child care, legal aid services, after-school clubs, marriage counselling, a workshop to train the handicapped, and many other social ministry areas. This has earned the respect of unbelievers around us and has provided openings for the gospel we would not otherwise experience.

With a heart for reaching the lost beyond Singapore, we have planted teams in Kazakhstan, Vladivostok, the Philippines, Indonesia, Hong Kong, and have ministered inside the 10/40 Window. Teams from our cell groups go out annually to minister in other parts of the world.

Our 'International Conference on the Cell Church' attracted over 1,400 Christian workers from 23 nations. Registrations came in so fast that we had to stop accepting new ones six weeks before the conference. We are anticipating sponsoring a 'Global Cell Church Conference' in 1996 in Singapore, which will be attended by 12,000 delegates from all over the earth.

The TOUCH EQUIPPING STATIONS SYSTEM was launched in 1992 with over 60 students, mostly from our own church. This ten-month training for zone pastors has now been expanded as we offer the videotaped courses to sister cell churches in other parts of the world. It is our desire to share all we have with others, and as a result 'TESS' is forecast to have centres on every major continent before the end of the century. Beginning in 1994, we have also started to provide an intensive month of training for Christian workers from all over the world who desire a more concentrated time to learn about the basic principles of the cell church. We were blessed with the presence of 105 from South Africa as well as others from Asia, Europe and the Americas. We are videotaping our teachers and developing voice-over sound tracks so TESS can be opened in sister cell churches around the world. Thus, translations of our materials and our videotapes are being prepared in Russian, Spanish, Cantonese and Japanese.

We have learned that there are seasons for harvesting those who have been cultivated by our cell group members. In December of 1993, we filled the 12,000 seat Singapore Indoor Stadium four times to accommodate those who wanted to see our 'Come Celebrate Christmas' musical. On Good Fridays, we have another form of evangelism as the cell groups meet in homes for a harvest time. The attendance at this special event numbers in thousands. Over 300 made first-time decisions on that one day. We function with the awareness that the harvests come after periods of seed-sowing and cultivating, and currently see three harvest cycles a year.

Our children's ministry has grown to contain 1,000 and we are currently launching inter-generational cell groups to minister to both the family and the cell groups. We are delighted to see the spiritual growth within the lives of our youngsters.

We built a four-storey building which includes a 1,400 seat auditorium, and paid cash for this $12,000,000 project. A recent survey of our stewardship has revealed that the giving of our members quite closely approximates a 100% tithe from all families, making our 1994 budget close to $10,000,000.

Our staff grows by the week. Now, with nearly 150 full-time employees, we have been blessed by a number of businessmen who have walked away from extremely high salaries to join us. Our West District pastor was previously a leading stock broker in Singapore. In an attempt to persuade him to remain at his post, his former employer gave him a Mercedes company car. On the last day at his job, he returned the keys of the car to his superior, who handed them back along with the title as a parting gift from the company! At the same time men, who had formerly driven large automobiles and now need to live on the lower income the church provides, take the bus to work.

We have established TOUCH Community Services as a neutral arm of our church to relate to the community. A magazine club, child care centres, latchkey clubs, legal aid services, support groups for diabetics, etc., now blanket the Republic. This has established goodwill for us among the many racial groups that live together in harmony in our nation. It also provides contacts with those who are searching for God, giving our cells entrances into groups of people we would not otherwise meet.

A special ministry of TOUCH Community Services is our training centre for those who are handicapped because of mental retardation or physical disorders. Skills are taught and employment is provided free of charge. Many of our graduates are now able to function effectively in jobs, including the maintenance of our own facilities. A ministry to the deaf has created cell groups among those who cannot hear sounds but who are open to hear the voice of God.

We have also added to our 'root system' into the unconverted world about us the implementation of interest groups. Each cell group sponsors a team of three of their best equipped members to form an interest group team. After being trained, they make contact with 1,000 homes through flyers placed in mailboxes. Interest groups reach those interested in guitar playing, marriage arranged yourselves, tennis, biking, etc. and also lonely people. Those who respond are grouped in a ratio of two unbelievers to one cell member for a 10–week encounter. Through this penetration into families across the island, our vision is to see converts worshipping in every block of flats in the Republic by the year 2000.

Beginning in 1995, TOUCH international (TI) will be launched by us, offering to each area of the world a network of cell churches who can encourage and assist each other in the task of bringing to this generation the good news of Christ's love. As this is written, centres have already been established in the United States, Russia,

Hong Kong, and Africa. Each TI centre will offer seminars, a magazine, equipping books and materials, etc. Through this ministry, we will seek to assist many other Christian groups to make the shift from tradition-bound church life to basic Christian communities.

CHAPTER 11

Blackburn Baptist
Choosing to Live

Pastor Stuart Robinson

Blackburn Baptist Church, Melbourne, Australia

The multi-level shopping centre was new, bright, clean, well-lit, fashionably decked out, and finely tuned with the latest piped music. It was tinselled to attract shoppers and their money. The trouble was that it also attracted problems as old as humanity whenever we cluster in cities.

Gangs of high school drop-outs started to assemble. At first, it was for the fun of seeing who could steal the most from the shops. Then it was for more violent clashes against one another. The local press highlighted the problem. Centre security guards and the state police seemed almost helpless to change the situation.

Then the 'God lady' and her helpers from Blackburn Baptist Church infiltrated the battle zone.

Blackburn is a comfortably quiet, middle-management, tree-lined dormitory suburb, twenty-five kilometres east of Melbourne's central business district. Urban sprawl washed over it in the post World War II building booms of the 1950s and 1960s. By the early 1970s the wave had moved on further eastward. The new housing fringes are now thirty kilometres beyond us.

In our part of the world, churches seem to pass through three phases; growth, maintenance and terminal. The growth phase usually lasts for the first twenty-five years. During this phase the church grows by people transferring into it as it is located in a newer suburb. Then transfer growth is replaced by biological growth as the children of earlier transferees grow, come to faith and join the church. The growth phase is ultimately replaced by the maintenance phase, which normally lasts for about twenty years. During this time children grow up, marry and move out, as it is usually too expensive for younger ones to buy into their parent's suburbs. Those who remain opt for security and the status quo. Evangelism slackens to occasional events which are more relevant to the congregation than to any outsiders. Numbers plateau and gradually start to decline.

This usually results in the terminal phase in which an increasingly ageing church membership lulls itself comfortably into a predictable end – the death of the church.

As a forty-year-old church, with churches closer to the centre of the city already closing, Blackburn Baptist realized a few years ago that it was settling into comfortable middle age. Its facilities were full. Its population was ageing. Although it had become one of the larger churches in the nation, it had plateaued and was starting to decline.

Without a vision for its future in God it was starting to lose momentum. It was starting to think about how things used to be rather than what they could be. It was boasting of the Lord but carefully avoiding having to be in the position of putting him to the test. It had little to keep it on its toes or drive it to its knees.

1992 was its year to refocus and redefine its vision for the future.

Its vision is now defined to become by the year 2000:

A CARING COMMUNITY – 2000 people
OF PRAYERFUL PEOPLE – 20% in weekly corporate prayer

EMPOWERED – by the Holy Spirit and through training and equipping
AND MINISTERING – 80% in small groups
IN MELBOURNE AND BEYOND – 100 staff at home and overseas plus 3 more daughter churches to be planted in Melbourne.

To bring the future into the present, the church first had to face the inadequacy of its facilities and their current location. We were faced with four options:-

1. Do nothing
2. Divide the fellowship
3. Expand current facilities
4. Relocate

Two daughter churches had already been planted and we could not expand further where we were.

To relocate and rebuild would cost millions of dollars. The church was challenged:-

- to concentrate not so much on what others might think but only upon what God might be saying.
- to separate clearly the necessity of making right decisions from the problems and pressures which might flow from this.
- to be prepared to face the impossible, knowing that with time, it will become possible.
- to exercise bold faith.

Relocation is now underway. Even though about 25% of the members left following the relocation decision and we are working through the deepest economic recession with record unemployment in living memory, the congregation has doubled its giving in the last three years.

Plans for a bigger 'sheep shed' to house our community have been completed. Construction at a new site is about to begin.

Regardless of geographical location, corporate and personal prayer is an essential sign of every growing church. Blackburn Baptist has met for prayer at 6 a.m. six days a week and at many other times weekly since 1985.

Since we cannot grow and transplant faster than we can develop leadership, in 1994 we appointed staff to establish the church to be more of an equipping centre, offering a range of options for the newest babe in Christ right through to those who are tracking to be our next generation of church planters and cross-cultural workers. Each course is designed to be a cognitive, emotional and spiritually transforming experience to produce future servant leaders.

The church bulletin declares that our purpose is 'To Know Christ and to Make Him Known'. It lists various key members of staff and then adds 'ministers – all the members'. All are expected to be in ministry according to their gifting. All ministry is carried out through small groups. Most committees have also been turned into communities of small groups. We are not just a church which has small groups. We are small groups which come together to be a church. This 'meta-model' allows for infinite expansion. Whether the groups are for fellowship, Bible study, homeless youth shelters, rapid response for community needs, the Board of Missions which oversees the church's 35 international staff in 12 countries, or whatever, all is done through small groups.

To adjust to its new future, the church has restructured, refocused and decided to live – even though the birth process has been slow and painful.

A new church is emerging. An evangelical church is slowly becoming evangelistic in word and deed. It is starting to turn itself inside out to live more on behalf of those who have yet to hear the good news it proclaims.

When a Melbourne daily newspaper interviewed our local shopping centre gangs, they replied, 'The police couldn't help us. The local social workers couldn't help us. Only these people from Blackburn Baptist Church have helped us by getting us off drugs, crime and violence and into a new way of life.'

As we helped these reformed gang members take back trailer loads of stolen goods to the shops and stood by while forgiveness was asked for, shop proprietors and security guards could hardly understand what was happening. When just one of the last 150 new converts took back what he had stolen, all he was left with was his underpants and socks. But within a day other kids had collected $500 to completely reclothe him.

When a church decides to live, Jesus is right there among the action.

CHAPTER 12

Wesley Mission Church, Sydney, Australia The World's Most Amazing City Church!

REVD DR GORDON MOYES

Superintendent

There are many great churches in the world. One in Seoul, Korea has more than half a million church members. That church's growth is built around 10,000 home groups where people are constantly witnessing to others.

In Nigeria, more than 80,000 people attend services emphasizing the miraculous. At a Methodist Pentecostal church in Santiago, Chile, more than 2,000 instruments form the orchestra. These are truly incredible churches built upon gathering large numbers of people to worship.

Yet, Wesley Mission, in the heart of Sydney, Australia, has the widest ministry of any church anywhere in the world.

This one church is responsible for:

- a ministry of psychiatrists and a hospital dealing with the emotionally ill,

- 400 people engaged in counselling the troubled and those in crisis,
- speaking to the entire nation through television, radio, and film,
- building significant relationships with the larger businesses in the land,
- providing beds and food for tens of thousands of people each year,
- providing accommodation for more than 2,000 people including babies, children, youth, families, and aged people every night of the year,
- training disabled people in social skills, and unemployed people in job skills,
- nursing dying cancer victims and caring for children with AIDS,
- training young people in creative arts for ministry, and house building for the poor,
- supporting the prisoner,
- confronting the politicians,
- teaching business management to corporate executives,
- serving a million meals a year to the needy,
- providing 4 million garments of clothing to those who cannot afford regular prices.

We have also recently completed one of the biggest building projects on church land undertaken anywhere in the world. The project included a $320 million dollar, thirty-eight storey office tower which is currently leased to developers to pay for construction costs, and used by the church as its head office. Areas are leased also to provide funds to cover the church's administration. The tower includes a theatre, church, and an auditorium seating more than 2,000 persons used by three different congregations simultaneously for daily worship as well as Sunday congregations, and also a public restaurant and classrooms for more than 1,000 members in study programmes of more than 150 classes a week.

The ministry areas cost some $40 million and were opened free of debt! There were thirty-two opening celebrations attended by 35,000 people. The annual Christmas pageant is attended by over 50,000 and is telecast internationally. This is indeed an amazing ministry!

This one church expresses itself through 45 services of worship each week in many different languages reaching out to ethnic communities. It is vigorous in church planting and has planted more than a dozen daughter congregations in the last decade.

It conducts its ministry in more than 300 buildings in eighty different suburbs and has assets of hundreds of millions of dollars dedicated to the ministry of the poor and needy. When this church speaks on social issues, governments listen. Everything is dedicated to serving the poor and proclaiming the word.

THE MINISTRY OF WESLEY MISSION SYDNEY, AUSTRALIA

Hundreds of thousands of people enter the arenas of the ministry of Wesley Mission each year. Hundreds of pastors from across Australia and from around the world come to learn the church-growth principles practised here. Over 1,500 have attended the Summer Schools For Successful Ministry conducted by the Superintendent and his team.

As they enter the church's new headquarters, many people have declared they thought they were entering the lobby of one of the two international five-star hotels adjacent to the church. Others have compared it to the great shopping emporium next door – 'David Jones' – authoritatively described as 'the most beautiful store in the world'.

In the foyer and reception area you are greeted by uniformed staff and volunteers. All are young, bright and friendly and offer assistance. A tour guide offers to show you the vast complex.

To your right is Wesley Restaurant which hosts hundreds of city business people each day for breakfast, lunch, and dinner or for morning and afternoon teas.

Wesley Centre provides catering facilities for office functions and executive conferences through the restaurant and offers an up-market package for special meetings, celebrations and conferences. As you go further into the Centre you approach Wesley Church. This seats 500 and is the worshipping home of some of our Sunday and weekday congregations. Wesley Church is fitted with a new pipe organ, and a baptistry. It has retained the original stained glass windows which beautified the old Wesley Chapel previously on this site. A second public area opens off the same lounge area and is known as the Lyceum. This too is used for our Chinese and Rotuman worship services. Both the church and the Lyceum have multi-lingual translation facilities.

One level below are function and activity rooms, some large enough to contain several hundred people while others are designed for smaller groups and adult study classes. These activity rooms are planned for use seven days a week by our parish, Sunday School, midweek groups, School for Seniors and other forms of training and education.

This floor also houses all of the offices of the Pastoral Division. Here people come for counselling from the large pastoral staff, or for membership classes. Here are also the offices of Creative Ministries International, the only fully-qualified and certified graduate-level college in the arts in Australia. Some classes are taken in this complex which also houses music rehearsal rooms and areas for drama and dance.

The large Dunbar Library of 15,000 volumes offers reading and study facilities for church members in English and Chinese, and for all Creative Ministries International students. A modern kitchen completes this floor.

A major attraction of Wesley Centre is the 1,000 seat Wesley Theatre. This theatre is the home of Wesley Mission's larger congregations each Sunday and for many mid-week activities as a performing arts centre. Wesley Theatre has a large stage and music podium suitable for orchestras and drama and dance, a baptistry built into a side wall, multiple-translation equipment, a wide screen for film, slide and video presentation and a state of the art, electronic computerized system for sound and lighting.

The unique Christie Theatre Organ is built high into another wall of Wesley Theatre. This theatre organ is renowned across the nation. From the opposite glass wall, parents with small children can feel part of all services without the children disturbing the rest of the congregation.

All the items of furniture for Sunday worship have been specially designed and constructed to fit the decor of the theatre. Every single item has been donated by church members and friends. Outside the theatre doors are 374 underground car parking spaces for worshippers on the same area of land!

Just outside the main lobby of the theatre is a well-stocked kiosk with refreshments, a parish kitchen for low-cost meals for people on limited budgets, a fine bookshop and the John Lees Chapel for prayer and meditation. This whole area is fully equipped for thousands of visitors. Within two areas a score of telephone lines enable personal counselling following our national telecasts each week, and for special financial appeals through the media.

All these facilities and meeting areas are accompanied by open and spacious lounge areas in which visitors can relax. The whole Wesley Centre is easily accessible by the disabled through lifts, escalators and gentle ramps.

Above these levels is the massive office tower. One level is set aside and leased to outside commercial offices, which provides a million dollars a year income to help cover the costs of operating the Church office.

On another level are the offices of about 100 senior staff of the church, covering the church's ministry in more than 300 other buildings across the city. In these other buildings more than 1,900 full-time paid staff minister on behalf of the congregation. In addition there are more than 3,000 volunteers, all of whom have undertaken some training.

In 1977, the Central Methodist Mission became part of the Uniting Church in Australia, and then changed its name to Wesley Mission. A new superintendent, the Revd Gordon Moyes, was appointed and he has carried on the work that had been so magnificently accomplished by earlier superintendents. Since his coming the work has expanded incredibly into more than ninety suburbs of Sydney where in more than 315 centres and services, the ministry of practical care for the needy is expressed.

Apart from the major redevelopment of its mid-city church and office complex, another $100 million dollars was raised for land acquisition, buildings and the construction of new facilities for further community service. New initiatives in evangelism have been undertaken across the nation by television and radio, new programmes of support for village life in the Philippines and India started, and more than 150 new services for the poor established. All of these required the purchase of additional property and the appointment of new staff, and a sustained fund-raising programme beyond what had ever been attempted by a church before.

Today Wesley Mission gives thanks to God for the successful completion of all these major works, and at the height of its power looks forward to serving the needs of the community and witnessing to Jesus Christ.

The ministry of this single church is so wide-spread that few people ever get to see it. In ninety suburbs, in a dozen rural and inter-state areas, and in a number of countries overseas, this church conducts a wide-spread ministry. Yet everything it does is according to careful strategy and biblical precedent as it seeks to minister in both word and deed.

People who live in the heart of a great city need the elevating experience of worship. Those who have always lived outside a city cannot appreciate the dehumanizing influence of large city developments, crowded factory areas, impersonal streets and towering blocks of tenement buildings. When you live in an environment where concrete replaces lawn, where light poles replace trees, where factories shut off the sunset, and where the noise of traffic is the contemporary substitute for the song of the birds, it is hard to worship God. Yet, city people need to worship. And God desires us to worship him. When there is little beauty in the world about us except what we seek in the streets glistening after rain, or in the early light on roof tops, the church has a very special responsibility to provide a place for city people where their spirits can sing, and where their hearts are elevated in worship. Wesley Mission operates out of the environment of worship.

Worship is central to all we do. We were born in praise to God and today we find resources and strength for our total ministry through the worship experience of our people. If our people did not gather for worship, to hear the word of God and to proclaim the gospel, all point and purpose to all the good deeds of service we undertake would be lost. That is why every person employed by Wesley Mission must be a committed Christian and a member of a worshipping congregation.

In the centre of Sydney's central business district, the central experience of the thousands of people touched through the life and work of Wesley Mission, is the worshipping community.

It is precisely at this point that Wesley Mission is different from other great social welfare agencies operated by denominational boards of churches, government welfare services, or those other agencies for the community's good. These, while born in a Christian environment, have now lost their Christian witness.

Wesley Mission is unique in that it holds worship and service together. We hold as many worship services as we have centres of service. We proclaim on our worship bulletins every week, 'The end of worship is the beginning of service.' Service and worship are inextricably bound together. Over the century we have maintained an increasing involvement in the worship of God by the people who serve in his name.

Wesley Church is the home for a number of our congregations. This new 500 seat church in the heart of the city, built in 1991, is the successor to a famous small Wesley Chapel which was opened in 1934. For fifty years it provided a mid-city centre for worship. It was then demolished and rebuilt as part of a major redevelopment Wesley undertook in the heart of the city.

Every Sunday this church has been the centre of the worship of God for people who live in the inner city, for those who come and uphold this centre of worship for the benefit of others, for tourists and visitors, for folk down in the city from their normal country home, and for international visitors who find in a strange land a place where they can worship God and feel at home. For fifty years Wesley Chapel has been the main worship centre of the Methodist Church in the heart of downtown Sydney.

Services are held in Wesley Church every day of the week, not just on Sundays, for the benefit of those who work and live in the city. Each of those daily services provides a different emphasis and attracts a different congregation. One service, 'Sing and Praise', celebrates the goodness of God in music and song. The 'Healing Service' is a service of witness in word and laying on of hands with prayer for those who are ill.

'Lunchtime Inspiration' is a service to lift the spirit in worship and praise to God. 'Chapel-in-the-City' is a service of preaching the positive power of God to lift a person's life. 'Mid-City Communion' is a quiet and reflective communion service aimed at encouraging our personal devotion.

Here communion is shared, baptisms are held, weddings are celebrated, funerals are conducted and special services designed to minister to the office worker and shop attendant.

Wesley Theatre is the scene of the main worship services of Wesley Mission. It is strange to many that we did not build one large, beautiful church to seat everybody at one sitting. Our understanding goes against that common trend. We have multiple facilities for worship and over 45 services each week, each with a differing ethos and feel about them. Many have different theological emphases and other differing styles of worship. We offer a smorgasbord of worship experience. Here there is a service and a congregation to suit everyone's personal desires.

For 90 years Wesley Mission has used a theatre to proclaim the gospel of Jesus Christ every Sunday night throughout wars, depressions and times of affluence. Its congregations have been varied. Hundreds of people from the widest variety of social, economic, educational, ethnic and vocational backgrounds, joined together in one purpose to worship God and to proclaim the gospel of grace.

Over the years the 'Church-in-a-Theatre' has been the centre of prophetic preaching, of frequent controversy and of faithful proclamation. There have been times when the Methodist denomination felt somewhat ashamed that its major city place of worship should be a theatre, and at times the liturgical structure of the service was designed to make it more into a cathedral than a theatre. However, with one of the finest theatre organs in the country, a magnificent screen and all the facilities for first-class cinema operation, the Church-in-a-Theatre operated according to its name, it was a church worshipping in a theatre, and therefore used lighting, sound and the screen every week to effect. During the preaching and the reading of the Scriptures the verses are shown on the screen for people to follow. The success of this theatre as a centre of worship and evangelism was seen in the multiplying of crowded services throughout Sunday. When the decision was made to demolish the downtown properties, it was a unanimous decision of the membership to build a new theatre, a centre for the performing arts and a Convention Centre with state-of-the-art facilities which would house the church's major worship services.

Wesley Theatre congregations are probably the most egalitarian in the world. Here you will find literally professors and physicians, prostitutes and alcoholics, teachers and computer programmers, skid-row drunks and homeless teenagers, sitting side-by-side and hearing the proclamation of the gospel.

Stalwart Christians, who could have been much more comfortable in their own environment in their local suburban churches, have committed themselves to this service week-by-week to uphold the preaching of the gospel and to enable the message to reach those in the community who desperately need the power of God to renew them.

It is a fact causing rejoicing that on every Sunday for the past century lives have been changed, challenged and converted through the power of the gospel. One exciting development in the last two decades has been the development of ethnic congregations. From an early beginning of a handful of Pacific Island people, services have been conducted weekly in four languages, Fijian, Rotuman, Samoan and Tongan, and from that handful of people twelve vibrant congregations of Pacific Islanders meet weekly for worship, communion, cultural experiences and fellowship around the meal table.

In the last decade a service was started for Asian people and that international service has grown from strength to strength, especially since the arrival of Dr Tony Chi. Today every Sunday morning a congregation numbering one thousand from a variety of countries of origin meets in Wesley Theatre to praise God.

A Chinese Service meets separately to cater for hundreds of Chinese-speaking people. A Spanish Congregation was established and now thrives as a separate congregation of several hundred. An Indonesian congregation and Sri Lankan congregation have also recently developed.

'Massive Celebrations', our largest services, combining all our congregations for a special occasion, are held in the largest facility in the nation, or outdoors, such as when over 50,000 attend our Christmas Service and pageant. Wesley Mission believes that in every large city there is a significant number of people who are either resident within the central city area or its immediate environs, who live at their places of work, as nurses in hospitals, students in dormitories, or caretakers in large city buildings, who together with visitors to the city, international travellers, tourists in motels, businessmen in hotels, seamen on board ships at the docks, and ordinary people who week by week are not attached to a local suburban church, need to find a place to worship. Today through Wesley Mission thousands of people each week worship God. The church is the only centre in society that brings people together for worship, to encourage them to capture the feeling of transcendence in life, and to help them find resources to equip them for living.

Worship at Wesley Mission is the focal point of the Mission's life. In what for many people are the concrete jungles of the city streets, hands in prayer and praise are lifted because of the church's worship. The Mission supports a large team of ministers, deaconesses, pastors and pastoral assistants, who form the staff core of the pastoral care provided by the church. But with them is a large team of elders who visit the sick or those who live near them, to provide encouragement, support and prayer for members under their pastoral oversight. 'Christian Education' is essential for all Christians. The city church has a major responsibility in helping Christians grow in their spiritual faith. We are called not only to help people to come to know Christ, but to grow in maturity in him.

To help facilitate this, Wesley Mission has established a significant Christian education programme. Hundreds of children attend our Sunday school. Along with this Sunday school growth has been the development of a new 'Sunday All-Age Christian Education Programme' in which hundreds of people are engaged in Bible study and discussion groups each week.

Over one hundred people meet every Tuesday night in the 'College for Christians'. This college meets in an assembly where the superintendent leads in a half-hour teaching programme on the life and ministry of Jesus. Then a series of classes are conducted which are attended by the college students. These classes consist of new counsellors training for Lifeline, mature counsellors who are doing graduate studies, Bible study groups, a lay-preacher's course, a course for tele-counsellors, and different groups which, from time to time, meet as part of the college. This whole programme is designed to help those who want to grow in their biblical knowledge. Prominent theologian, Dr Alan Harley, has joined our staff with the specific task of building a significant programme of Christian education through the 'City College of the Bible', aimed at city workers, and meeting after work each week.

Members of the pastoral team, visiting lecturers, and other professional staff provide the leadership for the various small group programmes in this Christian education work.

To help provide resources for the Christian Education programme, a new library has been established in the Wesley Centre with more than 15,000 books, competently catalogued, to aid people in research and personal growth. A computer helps in cataloguing and loaning books.

Prophetic ministry is biblical, but never fully understood by most congregations. The most controversial aspect of the ministry of Wesley Mission over the years has been its bold proclamation on matters of social justice. A city church is in a unique position to see the injustices of society and to have the ear of the public. Frequently social action has been the result of the strong presentation of the prophetic word to our country.

Just as the prophets of old spoke out the word of the Lord according to the social evils of their day, Wesley Mission has spoken a word of rebuke, of guidance and of witness to the Christian message.

Earlier Superintendents did not exercise the prophetic ministry with as much controversy or strength as did Revd Dr Sir Alan Walker who very quickly gained a reputation for his controversial and hard-hitting stands. Sometimes the Mission lost support because of his prophetic utterances, and other times greatly gained. Under his leadership the 'Pleasant Sunday Afternoon', which provided musical and biblical content for people over many decades in the heart of the city became the 'Lyceum Platform' where, for a number of years, social issues were debated and examined by speakers from the Christian point of view. The message of this crusading platform was carried by radio to the people of Sydney.

In recent years radio and television have become over-populated with current affairs programmes and people making utterances on the social issues of our day, and the voice of the church is only one of many competing voices. The Mission decided to continue its social issues presentation with a changed format. Instead of finding fifty social issues each year to fight from the Lyceum Platform, the Mission chose to raise issues on television and radio where we have direct access to a large listening audience, and instead of criticizing what the government had done, to provide more materials for the government by way of submissions during the decision-making process rather than after it.

Submissions are made to federal and state governments on a wide range of social and moral issues, and in one senate select report a great deal of the Mission's submission was accepted ultimately as the federal government's report. Dr Keith Suter has recently rejoined the Mission and has quickly used his remarkable intellectual skills (he has two PhDs!) and deep Christian commitment to formulate new submissions on government policy.

However, public protests are still held when matters of importance are raised, and the new Wesley Theatre is still open to the church at large to be used for significant Christian protest.

One important aspect of the prophetic ministry is at the individual level. The church must speak on behalf of those whom society ignores or tramples. The poor, the confused, the hopeless, the homeless, the unemployed, the socially neglected, the physically ill are part of the constituency that is represented by Wesley Mission. These people have little voice in the community and against the bureaucracies, and although their need is real it is seldom heard. Someone needs to stand alongside them, and with all of its strength speak on behalf of the powerless.

Wesley Mission sees itself as the voice of the voiceless. Understanding, compassion, backed by specialist social research, provide the basis for Christian social action on behalf of those people in the community who have no muscle of their own.

To represent the powerless in the community requires a city church ministry with muscle. A powerless church is only another ineffective voice. The weight and size and strategic strength of Wesley Mission have been effective in helping people in their battle against State and Federal government bureaucracies, and on behalf of ordinary people caught up in legislative changes and political decisions, the Mission speaks to enable justice to be done.

Only a church in the heart of the city with a city on its heart can do that! The powerlessness of ordinary people caught up in the machinery of government, and the apathy of so many public servants, makes more urgent the role of Wesley Mission.

Personal political lobbying at the highest level by senior staff and close personal contact with politicians and public service bureaucrats means that ordinary people's needs can be helped, frequently by a simple telephone call to the right person.

Leadership training is also required of each member. Christians need to discover their spiritual gifts and then learn how and where they are to use them. God grants to each of us capacities and gifts, and each Christian has the responsibility to discover his or her gifts and allow them to be used for the benefit of others. Churches grow when each individual gift is recognized, encouraged and developed, and then applied in the work of Jesus Christ.

At Wesley Mission members of the church are encouraged to exercise their spiritual gifts. Many are trained in forms of leadership. Over the years the Mission has been engaged in leadership training but there is still much to be done in training elders for leadership in the local congregation, the training of lay preachers, staff orientation programmes and the training of volunteers. Wesley Institute For Ministry and the Arts is a university level Christian college in the arts and Christian leadership. Nearly two hundred full-time and part-time students and a very strong faculty of fifty-three, make up the College body.

It has schools in dance, drama, music, counselling, theology, missions, and visual arts. Students are trained by professionals in their special field, but all do core subjects from a Christian perspective.

The College is the first of its type to be fully accredited by both federal and state educational bodies. The first two-dozen graduates are working full-time in churches and the professions as performing artists. The potential of this College is enormous, especially as students from the Third World discover its standing and capabilities. Christian ministry is much wider than the pulpit ministry, and these Christians are trained to minister through the arts. The new Wesley Centre is designed to enable performing artists to have the finest facilities in making their presentations to the city. A 1,000 student secondary school has been purchased by Wesley Mission as the new campus for the Wesley Institute.

Evangelism is the heart-beat of Wesley Mission. The strategy of the early church was to disciple the nations by winning people in the centre of the cities. Paul had a very impressive strategy which took him to the most famous cities of the ancient world: Corinth, Antioch, Philippi, Thessalonica, Jerusalem, and mighty Rome. It was his calculated strategy to win the empire by winning the great cities in it.

Paul saw the cities as the decision-making centres, and their life as the civilizing force for the rest of the empire. His strategy was to win the empire by winning the cities. Over the centuries the church built great cathedrals dominating city squares, and church bells pealed across the city streets. In another era, the preaching from the pulpit of city churches had tremendous influence over the attitudes of people in the cities.

Today the church does not have any protected place in the life of the city. But it still has its charge to win men and women to Jesus Christ, and in a country like Australia where 86% of our people live in seven cities, to be effective in our evangelism of this country. To be nationally effective requires us to be effective in our evangelism of her cities, particularly Sydney. Greater Sydney, between Newcastle and Wollongong, houses one out of every three persons in Australia.

The Lord Jesus Christ has given us the church to proclaim his gospel to people in this community. Wesley Mission has been faithful to its ministry of evangelism.

There have been some Christian missions, both in Australia and overseas, that have changed from evangelism to welfare, and then from the provision of welfare to the seeking of justice. We are not critical of their evolution of concepts, but we believe that evangelism is still primary in our tasks, and that all other emphases are in association with it.

Consequently, Wesley Mission has lived by evangelism. We believe the church is the church only when it is the church in mission.

Every Sunday in the new Wesley Theatre, the message is a gospel proclamation encouraging people to consider the claim of Jesus on their lives. In the beautiful phrase of John Wesley, 'We offer Christ.'

It is always a matter of rejoicing when we see people stepping forward as an outward sign of their inward commitment to Jesus Christ. Since 1884 open air preaching has been a feature in the life of Wesley Mission, and over the years in varying degrees an open air witness has been maintained. Several of our elders and key lay people have been trained in the art of sharing their faith with people in their own homes, and regular home visitation is conducted under the oversight of the Pastoral Department where the faith is shared with others. Two centuries ago, the founders of our church found that the most effective way to reach people with the gospel of Jesus was to proclaim it loudly on the city streets. Today the most effective way is to proclaim it softly through television.

The Mission has accepted this task of evangelism through the media with serious resolve. Wesley Mission has the largest media ministry of any church in Australia, and the significant fact is that although the media is used to inspire and educate, to propagate Christian truth and to encourage believers, in all of the major television programmes, both 'specials' throughout the year and in the regular half-hour weekly programme seen nationally, there is opportunity for people to make commitments to Jesus Christ and to respond by ringing tele-counsellors who are at a central telephone point.

These tele-counsellors have been trained to use the Scriptures and to counsel people according to their needs, helping them to make commitments to Jesus Christ. Then literature is sent to them, and local churches are contacted so that they may be followed up and encouraged to come into membership with a local congregation. This is the only programme of its kind in Australia, and the only weekly programme like it anywhere in the world.

Approximately 1,000 people each year are counselled in making a commitment to Jesus Christ through television and radio programmes. This aspect of evangelism is unique to Wesley Mission, Sydney, and has proved in the years it has been operating to be a valued contribution to the churches outreach ministry.

Media outreach takes the message of the gospel across the nation. The apostle Paul was quick to utilize the highways of the ancient Roman world to take the gospel into all the known parts of the empire. In the 20th century those highways are magazines and newspapers, and the airways of radio and television.

Revd Dr Gordon Moyes has developed a national weekly television ministry such as neither the Mission nor any other church in Australia had ever had before. Under his leadership, Wesley Film Productions was set up to produce television documentaries on the New Testament.

'Discovering Jesus', 'Discovering Paul', 'Discovering the Young Church' and 'Discovering Israel' have pioneered the way for Christian television and video productions. The series have been screened nationally and have been sold to many overseas countries and translated into Italian, Spanish and Korean. Wesley Mission is the only church in Australia with a full-time communications division with its own public relations and media department. Every week we present 'Turn Round Australia', a half-hour Christian magazine programme that is aired nationally on sixty stations across the country. Every city and town in the nation can see this programme. A special teenage evangelistic programme 'SWORDFISH' is produced and screened both nationally and internationally.

At Easter and Christmas, special programmes are also taken by a much wider network of television stations. An estimated one fifth of the entire nation watches the one hour Christmas Day special screened across Australia on Christmas Day during prime time evening television. It is also featured on television in many countries of Europe and Africa. This is the only Christian programme to receive such wide coverage from Australia.

Every Sunday night, the Mission presents 'Sunday Night Live', on Sydney station 2GB Newstalk 873. This three-hour programme presents the best in Christian comment and interviews and over its ten years on-air is the most listened to talk programme in Australia on a Sunday night.

Five times a year we produce 'Impact', our 32 page colour magazine. 'Impact' covers news of Mission activities and features personal stories of conversion. Each issue also challenges the reader to consider the claims of Jesus.

Press releases are issued regularly on major issues. We believe it is important that the Mission speak out on issues of social concern as well as uphold the standard of the gospel of Jesus Christ.

Wesley Graphics, the Mission's own art department, provides the necessary high class artwork, photographic work and typesetting requirements for the Mission. Printed literature is made available for all who write and request it. A cassette ministry provides multiple cassette duplication of every Wesley Theatre service, and the immediacy of this service is seen as people leaving the service each Sunday night are able to buy cassette recordings of the very service in which they have just participated.

Although the communications division is only one of many activities within the life of Wesley Mission, it is the foremost producer of Christian programmes in Australia with an output that exceeds all other Christian programme producers. One highlight of the church's evangelistic ministry each year is Easter Mission. During nine days of Holy Week, the whole city is presented with an evangelistic programme which is conducted in the city streets, in Hyde Park, through special functions, a breakfast for businessmen and community leaders, a luncheon for business women, special services conducted before work, during the day and at evening, special musical, drama, film and concerts, specially prepared spots on radio and television programmes seen across the nations, a live hour long telecast from the Sydney Opera House, and the use of all of the facilities of Wesley Centre, including Wesley Theatre and Wesley Chapel.

The aim of this special week is to present as many people as possible with the true story of the meaning of Easter. Each year, we reach 60,000 people face to face with the message of Easter. The Easter Sunrise Service, is seen in all capital cities of Australia and the larger regional centres.

A Darling Harbour Christmas was a bold attempt to put the true meaning of Christmas into one out of every five homes in the nation. A tightly structured Christmas service was presented before a congregation of 30,000 people, each with their candle and carol sheet.

The Christmas story was told out by about 2,000 members of the cast and choir who became the people of Bethlehem. Craftsmen, potters, carpenters, weavers set the

scene. The shepherds arrived with their flocks of real
sheep. Mary and Joseph arrived with a donkey. The wise
men arrived on their haughty camels in splendid attire,
much to the delight of children. The colour and pageantry
caught the imagination of the country as we retold the
true meaning of Christmas – Handel's 'Hallelujah Chorus',
sung by the full choir and accompanied by a symphony
orchestra brought the evening to a climax, and as 'King of
Kings and Lord of Lords' was sung, a massive fireworks
display burst into the heavens. It was an awesome
experience!

As part of this presentation, viewers were asked to
contribute to the needs of those homeless with whom
we minister. Thousands rang our counsellors to make
donations and to speak about the coming of Christ.

Evangelistic outreach is also conducted by members of
the pastoral staff in other churches. As several members of
the pastoral staff have evangelistic gifts, there is a call
upon them by other churches to use their gifts in missions
and crusades. About eight crusades a year are conducted
in other churches with prayer, encouragement, and in
some cases through gifted members using their skills in
music, counselling or personal testimony. Students from
Wesley Institute are able to use their musical gifts in
supporting these ministries. One staff member has been
effectively conducting city-wide crusades in India, Sri
Lanka, and Eastern Europe.

The cutting edge of evangelism must be present in any
effective city ministry, and Wesley Mission has demonstrated over the past century that it is not enough for a
church just to worship or serve, but that there must be the
gospel of hope presented to those in the city streets.

Consequently, in the evangelistic programme of Wesley
Mission its services of outreach are designed primarily for
the person who is not a Christian.

Special effort is made to reach these people with the
good news of the gospel. These services are so arranged
that those people who are not Christians can understand
what is happening and feel at home during them.

Conversions are recorded. Lives are changed. The Mission has been true to the command of the Master to disciple people in his name.

(A fuller outline of the church's ministry is available in the book *MISSION ON!*)

CHAPTER 13

Faith Revival Church, Phoenix, South Africa

REVD LESLIE JAMES

Before being posted to my first pastorate, my prayer was that the church that I would pastor would not be an ordinary church which had only a few participators among many spectators. My first pastorate was Faith Revival Church in the suburb of Phoenix, north of Durban, South Africa in the year 1982. Since we could meet as a congregation only on Sundays, I firstly encouraged all my leaders to request school classrooms in all the districts of Phoenix so that we could begin mid-week fellowships. I then encouraged the formation of cell groups, and the factor that I emphasized most was growth. Cells had to continually divide and thus multiply. Within a short space of time we had 150 cell groups. I personally trained all cell leaders on Friday nights. They were given copies of their lessons for the week and we then prayed together till midnight.

Jesus said, 'If I be lifted up I will draw all men unto me.' As a church our aim was 'to lift Jesus up'. We did this through colourful float processions through the streets of Phoenix, through a massive billboard at the railway station and through intensive local evangelism. Within a short space of time, 4 years to be precise, we became (according to the Full Gospel Church Monthly magazine) the largest Indian church in South Africa. At this point in time our vision was strictly local. We knew that, 'God so loved the world . . .' but since our 'world' was Phoenix, Durban and South Africa we concentrated only on these areas. Through this ministry twenty-one workers were raised by the Lord to spread the gospel in other areas of South Africa.

However, a sponsored trip to the USA in July 1986 led to a chain of events which altered our course and destiny as a church. After a fruitful and delightful trip we returned to South Africa via Frankfurt, Germany. During my short stay in Frankfurt I had a life-changing experience. While I was reflecting on our blessings at home and the warm acceptance we received in the USA, I heard a voice say, 'What about those that never heard?' This was followed by three sleepless nights during which I constantly saw a multitude of outstretched hands. As I walked the streets of Frankfurt my heart was moved with compassion for the Turks begging on the streets and the passive people I encountered everywhere.

Although the Second World War was long over, a war of far greater intensity was being waged in the heavenlies for the utter destruction of these precious souls. When I returned to my local pastorate, I announced to the church that we no longer had a local mission but a world mission. This set in motion a chain of events which led to my decision to leave a thriving church with a tremendous work force and a congregation of over 8,000, eight 100–seater buses, a 10,000–seater tent, 2.5 acres of land, equipment and even my car, to be obedient to the heavenly vision. I began afresh in 1987 without the usual comforts and accessories or paraphernalia that characterize a local church, but with a strong nucleus of believers who were willing to seek the lost at any cost. It cost Jesus his life to save the lost and therefore it must also cost us everything we have.

We began our new work by encouraging prayer for

world evangelization. During this time we gathered information from newspaper articles, magazines and television news items. We had at that time no idea or personal experience of what the mission fields looked like. But an opportunity arose when we were invited to a Mozambican refugee camp in Gazankulu, South Africa. The encounter left us with a determination to put our hands to the plough in the mission fields of the world. One old woman's words still ring in my ears till this day. After we had presented the gospel message to her, she asked, 'When did this Jesus come?' I replied, 'Almost 2000 years ago.' She said, 'What took you so long? Why didn't you come with the good news earlier? If you had, my children and grandchildren who were torn apart by wild animals in the Kruger National Park, would have been alive today.' These words still haunt me.

After this trip and our exposure to the lostness of people, prayer for the lost millions of our land and the world took on a new fervency. The Lord of the harvest then reached down in our midst and separated 14 young people for missionary training. These faithful, zealous young people presented themselves for a time of vigorous training. As we continued in prayer for clarification of the call and vision, we realized that mission is not an option but a mandate for the whole church.

We were led during our times of prayer to pray for India; the sheer size of the population and the tremendous number of unevangelized people motivated us to pray for this land. It was during this time that I embarked on my first trip to India, to see for myself the condition of this mission field. On my return we continued to pray for world missions but concentrated our prayer effort on India and her various states.

January 1989 was an historic moment in our land when 14 young people took the gospel and headed for their motherland. A few years later we discovered that Operation World (1987 edition), a handbook for intercessors world-wide, contained a request for the South African Indian Church to take the gospel back to the motherland. At the time that we were changing course, we had no idea that it was in response to the prayer of God's people world-wide. At the same time I would like to add that these missionaries did not go because of the need in India, but in response to the command given in Matthew 28:19–20. The Lord of the Harvest reached into our midst and separated this harvest force. Since 1987 he has continued to lead and instruct us in this area.

Since the church was not in a position financially to support this missions endeavour, these missionaries looked to the Lord for their air fares and monthly support. He faithfully provided for every one of them. All glory to his name! 1989 was a year of trials and testings because the enemy was enraged by our audacity at invading his territory. We encountered opposition from every conceivable quarter. Because our battle was not against flesh and blood, we prevailed in prayer, stood our ground and declared the victory that Jesus had given us over all the enemy's works. Those who went out to the mission fields also experienced much tribulation because of their pioneering status. However because, 'Greater is he that is in us, than he that is in the world', they were able to triumph in every situation. During this time we made many costly mistakes through our ignorance but, because he has chosen us and we have not chosen him, his grace and mercy helped us to overcome every obstacle.

It would be in order at this stage to express the sentiment of a Christian professor from an Agricultural College in Rewa, Madhya Pradesh, India. He said that he had been praying for years for the Lord to send missionaries to the state of Madhya Pradesh and was overwhelmed by the arrival of the South African mission team. Together with other committed, zealous nationals he joined the missionaries in street and intense local evangelism. In February this year (1994) we were privileged to meet a couple who are medical practitioners from Belgaum, India who were saved through the ministry of the first mission team.

A never-to-be-forgotten experience awaited me in 1989 as I attended the Lausanne II conference in Manila. For the first time I realized that the body of Christ world-wide was listening to the same voice at the same time. This conference on world evangelization sharpened my vision and clarified my goals. Words fail to express the enrichment I received through this conference. On my return I encouraged the whole church to make itself available to the Lord of Missions. In October 1989 we invited local pastors and mission leaders from all parts of the country to attend the launching of the South African Global Network for World Evangelization. The response to this meeting was overwhelming. But as we continued in missionary intercession and prayer for the harvest fields at our local church, the Lord led us to the next step or phase of the ministry. He provided a building which could be used as a missionary training centre. When we negotiated for this building we did not have the finances to renovate it, equip it or install electricity and water services. But, by the time the building was prepared, the Lord provided the students and all the basic necessary equipment. To him be the glory, praise and honour.

In the first year (1991) 8 students were trained, followed by 10 in 1992, 10 in 1993 and now 14 in 1994. Of these, 10 missionaries are stationed in India, 2 in Taiwan and 2 in Malawi. In addition, 2 missionaries from the 1989 team are now serving in Namibia and a few more in South Africa. At the end of each year we hold a mission graduation ceremony at a renowned venue in the city. We invite pastors and Christian leaders from all denominations and fellowships in our city to this ceremony. Once again the motive is to mobilize Christ's church to evangelize the world.

The year 1993 marked yet another milestone in the history of our church when one of our missionary couples opened the William Carey School of World Missions in Madras, India. This opening coincided with the William Carey bicentennial celebrations in India. On July 9th,

1994 we will hold our first graduation of Indian nationals. One of the mission students from this school has already planted a church in his home village near Salem, the other 8 are expected to follow suit. Another of our missionary couples who lived in a village near Calcutta in 1993 baptized their first candidate in the village in January this year. Being the only English-speaking person in his village he responded to the gospel message by introducing his best friend and his uncle and aunt to Jesus.

Already 2 cells have been started in an unreached village. Our vision is to train 100 missionaries at home and another 100 in India every year. Within 2 years, plans are already at an advanced stage for the launch of our mission school in Zambia. The missions message and vision have been kept alive in the hearts of our local congregation through the constant flow of fresh missionary information provided by visiting missionaries and mission leaders. The following are some of the international speakers who shared the burden of missions at our local fellowship:

Revd Panya Baba (1988)
John Robb (1989)
Dr Thomas Wang (1990)
Patrick Johnstone (1992)
Dr John Richard (1993)
Revd David Bliss (1994)

The local congregation has the opportunity to serve as senders by contributing to the mission fund every Sunday morning. And with these funds we have been supporting all our missionaries at home and abroad.

When Jesus took the loaves of bread and fish, he firstly blessed them, then broke them and fed them to the multitudes. In a similar manner he firstly blessed us, broke us, and now he is feeding us to the multitudes. And all we want to be is a church committed to reaching the lost at any cost. We did not have financial resources, qualified personnel, mission training and any experience on the mission fields; but what we did have was a vision for the lost. And how do you get this vision?

I believe much prayer and travail for the lost produces this vision. 'Without vision the people perish.' May the Lord help us not to lose this vision.

CHAPTER 14

The Great Commission and the Dutch Reformed Church Rondebosch 1994

DR ERNST VAN DER WALT

The Dutch Reformed church of Rondebosch, with mainly Afrikaans speaking members, was established just over a century ago in the southern suburbs of the fairest Cape. Comparing its membership with other churches in the Cape Peninsula and elsewhere in South Africa, Rondebosch is not a large congregation. For a period of 79 years until 1989 Rondebosch was the church of the prime ministers and latterly the presidents while parliament was in session in Cape Town. My relationship with the Rondebosch church commenced almost twelve years ago when I was called to this church. Even at that time, our church, through the involvement of a member Hettie Hugo, had a good working relationship with Operation Mobilization of South Africa, an international missions organization with the logo 'Exciting God's people to finish the task of world evangelism', recruiting long and short-term missionaries to bring the good news to the unreached peoples of our world. One of the most successful evangelism strategies of OM is the outreach through the well-known mission ships, Doulos and Logos II and the latter's predecessor Logos.

HETTIE HUGO – AN OCCUPATIONAL THERAPIST BECOMES CHRIST'S MISSIONARY

Hettie Hugo, a young occupational therapist with a lot of initiative and a member of our church, had already joined the Doulos in September 1981 when we arrived in Rondebosch. The Lord called her some time before and she accepted the challenge. For more than two years she travelled to distant ports and cities of the world with the good news of God's love for the world. One of the greatest miracles she experienced was to see her own heart opening up more and more to the needs of people which she was unaware of; being concerned about them, taking care of them both physically and spiritually, loving them with a genuine love.

Responding to the vast numbers of people in need was an overwhelming challenge but a wonderful privilege to accept. The Doulos experience exposed not only Hettie to world evangelism, but also a group of home church supporters who received her prayer letters and prayed with great enthusiasm for this young missionary on the frontier. Her mission also broadened the vision of her home church to become people of God with a world mission perspective. Now, eleven years later, after she has married a French Canadian, Normand Saindon, and with three beautiful children, her heart is still aflame for Jesus her Lord, and his last command to bring the good news to the unreached. After Hettie and her husband had ministered to drug abusers in Montreal in Canada for a couple of years they moved back to Cape Town for full-time ministry in missions.

JOAN THERON – JESUS CHRIST'S NURSE

Joan Theron, an energetic young sister at the Red Cross Children's Hospital, and a committed deacon in our church, was a friend of Hettie Hugo. The reports and prayer requests of Hettie made an impact on her life to become more than a distant supporter of world missions. Eventually the Lord convinced her also to take the good news to the unprivileged. She joined the crew of the Logos as a nurse and with the other OM-ers visited many ports in South America to bring hope and new life. Joining the ship committed her to evangelizing the people living in and around harbour cities through a variety of methods and bringing a message of hope many times through a Spanish interpreter, street dramas, sketch-board drawings, songs and visits to local churches and friendship evangelism. After an exhausting ministry of a couple of years Joan returned to her home church.

As the Lord had moulded her into a missionary with a heart and an eye for the lost, she accepted a combined post as a nursing sister-cum-social worker in a consortium of farms growing apples in the district of Ceres, an up-country town. Here her main focus was on the women and children of the apple packers. She cared for their physical and spiritual well-being. As a loving, caring person she demonstrated the love of Jesus Christ to the sick and the seeking. She applied the biblical discipleship method which she learned at OM on board the Logos. The Lord blessed her ministry tremendously. The process of multiplication started with the teenage coloured girls in the Ceres Koue Bokkeveld area. At least one of these girls joined OM also to become a missionary with a message of hope to the world.

Joan married Wessel van der Merwe, a young Afrikaans speaking farmer who loves the Lord. After they had prayed about their mutual future the Lord called them to the devastated land of Mozambique. Mozambique was a Portuguese colony for centuries until its independence a couple of years ago. A severe and bloody war started between Frelimo and Renamo, ruining the country and leading to the death of thousands of people. Thousands of inhabitants of Mozambique fled for their lives to neighbouring countries, many with only the few possessions which they could carry with them. The people of Mozambique were crying out for help. These were the people to whom God called Wessel and Joan. The war was still on and every night the sound of automatic weapons could be heard. Because of land mines many roads were unsafe. But in spite of the dangers, the love of Christ motivated this couple to go. Initially under very difficult and dangerous circumstances as part of an OM team, they started a mission station at Xilembene in the southern region of Mozambique. There was no building, no sewerage system, no facilities whatsoever. The people speak Swahili as their first language and some Portuguese as their second language. Both were new languages to Joan and Wessel, but they were motivated and faced up to these new cultural challenges. They used interpreters to communicate the message of hope. The inhabitants of Xilembene welcomed them with open arms. The Lord opened their hearts to the gospel which they received with enthusiasm. A church was planted and started to grow. Joan took the responsibility for a health clinic as well as a women's discipleship group. Large teams of young people from South Africa accepted the challenge to visit Mozambique on summer and winter campaigns. The Jesus film particularly is an effective evangelism tool. Many people from Mozambique have been overwhelmed to see 'Jesus being crucified'. Up to 1994 between 200,000 and 250,000 Mozambique people have been reached by the gospel during the last couple of years' ministry. A peace accord was signed between the two warring factions and the following day the shootings stopped. More than one tragedy has occurred lately. Issy Volschenk, one of the team members, died during 1994 of malaria. The team leader at Xilembebe, Raymond Robyn and his wife had a very serious motor-car accident. In addition, Wessel, Joan's husband, contracted malaria while he was the acting team leader! By the grace of the Lord he has now regained his health and is continuing his ministry in Xilembene with great enthusiasm.

ERNST VAN DER WALT JUNIOR –
GEORGE VERWER'S 'GO-FOR'

My eldest son, Ernst van der Walt junior, joined OM in 1989 after he had finished his school career and his military training. After attending 'Love Europe', a big and challenging missions conference in Germany he joined the international office of OM in Bromley near London. He became the 'go-for' of George Verwer, the international director and founder of OM. For the following twelve months he had a couple of very interesting experiences in the dynamics of OM. On more than one trip he accompanied George to Scotland, Wales and centres in England to help mobilize Christians for mission. One of his responsibilities was to meet missionaries at one of London's airports. Eventually after a period of twelve months he finished his ministry in Bromley and came home to share his experiences with his home church at Rondebosch. The Lord no doubt gave him a new vision of the world-wide perspective of his great commission.

His next move was to the World Mission Centre run by professor Ralph Winter, the founder and world mission pioneer, in Pasadena, California, USA. No stumbling block prevented him from going to the initiators of world missions in modern times. He arrived in Pasadena, enrolled for the course in Religious Studies and he received his diploma in 1992. His concern for the unreached people was the primary reason for his joining the AD2000 office in Pasadena and eventually in Colorado Springs where he became part of the preparation team for GCOWE '95 in Seoul, South Korea. After a couple of months he left with the intention of upgrading his academic qualifications at the University of Stellenbosch. He enrolled for a degree in economics to equip himself better for his task in missions management. Although he enjoys his course in the world of commerce, his major interest continues to be the mission of the Lord. He attended the first national steering committee meeting of

AD2000 in Durban after a night's travel on a motor-bus, a distance of more than 1,600 kilometres.

ERICA BIEHLER – ANOTHER OCCUPATIONAL THERAPIST BECOMES A MISSIONARY

Erica Biehler, an occupational therapist, joined a few short-term outreaches of OM where the Lord changed her heart according to the words of the song:

I want to serve the purpose of God in my generation.
I want to serve the purpose of God while I am alive.
I want to give my life for something that will last for ever.
Oh, I delight to do your will.
What is on your heart?
Show me what to do,
Let me know your will and I will follow you.

These words became the prayer of Erica's heart. She still owed part of her study loan when she decided to take a step in faith as a 'tentmaker' and start a part-time private practice as occupational therapist and become a missionary in her local church, Rondebosch. Her goal was to develop a mission awareness in local churches in and around Rondebosch.

She made stimulating posters and decorated the church notice-board beautifully with interesting information about our mission-fields. One of these mission-field exhibitions, where one of our members went to work with drug addicts, was the most interesting island of Sri Lanka, formerly known as Ceylon. At regular intervals Erica changes the exhibitions. Through these exhibitions our church members were able to 'visit' countries like Swaziland, Mozambique and France where missionaries went to bring the good news to the unreached. These exhibitions provide an opportunity for church members to 'meet' our missionaries and to see the reality of their environment where they minister as real people with real struggles and real victories for Jesus Christ. The aim of this project is to enthuse more members to pray for our missionaries with specific needs and to encourage people to write letters to these missionaries.

God provided an open door to become part of the Love Europe mission conference and thereafter to be part of the outreach in Romania. It was shortly after the Lord lifted the iron curtain, and to see the hunger and the thirst of the people of Romania was an experience beyond words. What a wonderful privilege to be part of God's answer to these unfortunate people in the former East bloc countries. Erica committed herself to read as many news and prayer-letters of missionaries she could lay her hands on in order to get a clearer picture of God's work in our world of today. The newsletter 'Pulse' is a very useful instrument to update our prayer cards that we use at our early Sunday morning prayer meeting. Some statistics, needs and information bits are published in the weekly church bulletin and monthly newsletter. The administration of a regular programme on missions on Radio Pulpit, a Christian radio station, was another opportunity which the Lord provided. Many short-term missionaries joined OM because of these programmes.

A next challenge was to mobilize a couple of our church members to visit a mission field in Swaziland to see and experience the needs of a family with whom we have a close relationship. What an eye-opener to experience the demands of cross-cultural mission work and to see the joy and appreciation of missionaries who serve the Lord under lonely circumstances! Never again can interceding for these people on the frontline be vague and unspecified. A new spirit of caring was created.

The next challenge for Erica was to commit herself to a full-time ministry for the Lord by accepting the responsibility of the administration of an evangelism programme for churches in the Western Cape. She finally terminated her occupational therapy career in order to make her skills and experience available to Christians, assisting them to share their faith in Jesus Christ with others. The responsibility of the first regional director of Evangelism Explosion in South Africa became her ministry. An important responsibility in this ministry is to support Christian leaders who are training members of their local churches.

At the beginning Erica says the Lord had to help her to overcome her inability to share her faith with others. She got involved in the local church outreach programme of Evangelism Explosion. Reaching out with the gospel of Jesus Christ meant a lot to her and she developed a longing to get involved in helping believers to be trained in practical evangelism.

She writes: 'And as the time goes by, I get even more excited about our God sharing his love with us and changing us to be channels of this love to reach others.'

HELENA VAN DER WALT – A MOVER OF MOUNTAINS IN THE MUSIC MINISTRY FOR JESUS

Our only daughter, Helena van der Walt, received her BComm degree at the end of 1993 at the University of Stellenbosch. For many years, one of the highlights of the university has been the Mission week during the month of August where thousands of students attend and take part. In 1992 Helena took the responsibility of fund-raiser for the Missions Week Committee. With an unsurpassed dedication she started to generate finances. The international speaker for this well-planned occasion was Edison Quero. He made a great impact on his audience of young students. A few hundred of these attendees made themselves available to fulfil the great command of Jesus.

During Helena's final year, Bill Drake, the music director of OM, visited South Africa for the first 'Love Southern Africa' Conference in Wellington. We hosted Bill at our home in Cape Town. Helena was deeply touched by Bill's music ministry, his commitment to Jesus Christ, the beauty of the lyrics of his songs, and the way he interpreted the beautiful music he wrote himself. She was willing to consider the possibility of joining the music ministry in South Africa.

When Helena obtained her degree she was absolutely convinced that the music ministry for Jesus was her calling. She started a promotion programme for Bill Drake's CDs and cassettes. She visited church youth groups and enthused many a teenager with Jesus' love for the unsaved. Bill planned to visit Cape Town for a big youth rally and concert in Stellenbosch. Helena was the manager, funds generator and organizer. She lived with her parents initially with almost no income. Her commitment, perseverance and trust in Jesus to provide was something unbelievable! No disappointment could stop her. She was convinced that this was the Lord's plan for her life at this stage. More than one miracle materialized. The Lord provided for every need. Bill arrived and was overwhelmed by the detail of the planning of his young dedicated manager. The evening of the concert became a reality. More than 4,000 teenagers from many cultural backgrounds were fascinated by Bill's songs of obedience to the Lord and the willingness to reach out to the unreached. The climax of the evening was when more than 4,000 teenagers on their knees sang the words of Bill's song 'I'll obey':

> I'll obey and serve you,
> I'll obey because I love you,
> My life is in your hands
> For it's the way to prove my love,
> when feelings go away.
> If it costs me everything,
> I'll obey.

THE HUDSON FAMILY – ON THEIR WAY TO KYRGYSTAN

Robert Hudson of the Meadowridge Baptist Church realized that the Lord was calling him to the unreached of the 10/40 Window. He and his wife committed themselves and they are in training at YWAM SA to leave their country later in 1994 on a cross-cultural long-term outreach to the people of Kyrgystan. The AD2000 movement was started in South Africa at the end of 1993.

One of the regional committees was started in Cape Town shortly afterwards. The number one goal of AD2000 is to provide information about the unreached people groups and to network churches. While the unreached track did some research on the needs of the unreached, they became aware of Roger Hudson's urge for the people of Kyrgystan. The Meadowridge Baptist Church, in collaboration with the Dutch Reformed Church of Rondebosch and other churches, are planning to be the Hudson's senders to the unreached people of Kyrgystan in a mutual mission effort.

In addition to these we have Pieter ter Haar ministering in Sri Lanka with the drug addicts, Kobus van Zyl, a leader of a small team of young people who are reaching out during 1994 in Kenya, and the old faithful, Etta Langenhoven, who sold thousands of rand's worth of fruit rolls during the last years to help support our missionaries on the frontiers financially.

We are experiencing the richness and abundance of the Lord's blessings. We are re-committing ourselves for the challenge ahead of us to co-ordinate with other churches in getting the gospel to the ends of the earth in our eagerness for the second coming of Christ.

CHAPTER 15

The Holy Ghost Revival Centre, Accra, Ghana

M. ASAMOAH-MANU
Church Secretary

The Assemblies of God Holy Ghost Revival Centre is committed to the concept: 'A Church for Every People and The Gospel for Every Person by The Year 2000'.

Our congregation is in Dansoman, a suburb of Accra, the capital of Ghana. The Assemblies of God has over eighty churches within the Accra-Tema metropolis, with an average growth of about fifteen churches a year within the region. There is a programme by which sister Assemblies of God churches within a geographical location of the metropolis pool their resources to plant new congregations annually, and our church has been involved. In addition to this, the Holy Ghost Revival Centre has other programmes for ensuring 'A Church for Every People and The Gospel For Every Person By The Year 2000'.

PERSONAL EVANGELISM

The Pastor conducts periodic personal evangelism teachings to equip the members for personal soul-winning.

Gospel tracts are issued to the members periodically to enhance their evangelistic thrust.

LIFE GROUP

Our congregation adopted a programme by which church members within a particular vicinity met weekly for prayer and Bible discussion. It is codenamed LIFE – an acronym for:

L – LOVE (practical expression of concern for one another)
I – INSTRUCTION (through Bible discussion)
F – FELLOWSHIP
E – EVANGELISM

The aim of the LIFE group clearly stands out from the meaning expressed above. Evangelism among the residents of a particular LIFE group's neighbourhood is an important obligation. The LIFE groups also help to follow up those who visit our church and help to nurture them in Christ. As a group grows beyond fifteen members it has to divide.

CHILDREN'S MINISTRY

Our church has a growing children's ministry. This is helping street children to find Jesus as Saviour.

By all these measures, our local congregation is reaching the unreached people within the catchment area of the church. But, apart from these, we are also reaching other people for Christ through our Missions programme.

MISSIONS

1. Muslim Outreach Support

The alarming rate at which Islam is spreading is of great concern to our congregation. Apart from the fervent prayer for ministries among Muslims, our congregation gives monthly financial support to one minister who pastors a church for converted Muslims at Abakrampa in the Central Region of Ghana. We have provided a gas lamp and a number of benches for the church. The pastor, Ben Wahab Adams, is currently working at evangelizing other Muslim-dominated communities in the Central Region of Ghana.

2. Unreached Ethnic Communities

Our local congregation is also involved with Peoples Group Outreach.

(a) Kasena Peoples Church

We are supporting a church founded exclusively for the Kasena-speaking people who live within and around Achimota and Domi (suburbs of Accra). We give monthly financial support and provide other logistics as and when the needs arise. These people are from the Upper West Region of Ghana who have migrated to the south mainly due to economic reasons. They are unlettered and pre-dominantly idol-worshippers. Brother Anthony Kukpoi works full-time among these Kasenas. He started with an adult literacy programme and now there is an Assemblies of God church among them.

(b) Sisala Church

Our church has also adopted a church in Tumu in the Upper West Region of Ghana. Tumu is the traditional capital of the Sisala people who are among the major unreached ethnic groups in the Upper West. The Holy Ghost Revival Centre has provided gas lamps, benches, musical instruments and other logistics in addition to paying the monthly salary of the resident pastor, Edward Apam.

Our local church also gives monthly and periodic

financial support to para-church and other Christian organizations in Ghana. In addition, we sponsor people through Bible School education.

All this financial support is possible because our pastor has taught the members to give to missions. On the first Sunday of every month, every member gives a special offering to missions. Ironically, our local church does not have its own place of worship. We are presently worshipping in a rented building as we work towards acquiring land to put up a church building; but we are supporting a missions programme because we believe that the salvation of man should be the greatest need that the church must address. God will help us as we help others.

FUTURE PLANS

We plan to open a church in an unreached village within the Greater Accra Region in 1995 and use the doctors and nurses in our congregation to introduce a primary health care programme there. This will be an effort into a holistic ministry programme.

To this end, we plan to step up our role as 'the home church' of GHACOE Women's Ministry. GHACOE is the acronym for Ghana Congress on Evangelization. It is primarily a Women's Ministry pursuing a holistic programme for women, the poor, and a concern for the environment. GHACOE, whose headquarters is located at Asoredanho, has selected our church, the Holy Ghost Revival Centre of the Assemblies of God, as their 'Home Church'. GHACOE's goal is to equip and present women complete in Christ by providing physical, moral and spiritual balance to women in Ghana, and through their networking programme, develop leadership qualities and talents of women in Ghana and other countries in Africa through short and long-term holistic programmes which include income-generating ventures. Most of the participants in the programmes consist of potential women leaders drawn from all regions in Ghana and a number of other countries in Africa. While they are on their programmes in Accra, these participants use our church as their 'Home Church'. We plan, in the coming year, to strengthen this relationship with GHACOE, by following-up on the GHACOE converts.

These are our contributions towards ensuring 'A Church For Every People And The Gospel For Every Person by the year 2000'.

CHAPTER 16

St James Church, Kenilworth, South Africa

REVD A. S. THOMAS

During 25 years of ministry in St James Church Kenilworth, we acknowledge that the ever present hand of God has been very evident through many unbelievers committing their lives to his Son, the Lord Jesus Christ, as their personal Saviour. Above all things reverence for God's word has directed men, women and children into the ways of God and spiritual development has encouraged people from all walks of life to serve and honour the name of Jesus.

From humble circumstances in August 1968 this church has grown from 22 people, attending the first church service, to 4,000 people passing through the church services today on an average Sunday. Children have also been a special consideration and a Sunday School starting with 11 children has mushroomed into one with 800 children and this does not include the youth, numbering many hundreds, who attend weekend clubs and their own special teen-church.

When accommodation was not sufficient for the growing congregations, the local civic centre was used, graduating to a cinema and ultimately to a theatre seating 2,500. This auditorium was regularly packed and open to all who wished to hear the word of God.

The little chapel of St James obviously needed to be extended, and this was done in a piecemeal way. The district had changed character. Flats had been erected and old houses turned into up-market cottages that attracted the young professionals. To attract the newcomers many innovations needed to be introduced. To music was added drama and films.

Outreach into the community by knocking on doors and saying 'Just come as you are now!' resulted in many attending church and many staying and becoming members.

The growing congregations and the development of the many supporting departments put great pressure on space. People were coming from all over the Peninsula and further afield. It was apparent that St James Church in the Kenilworth area was at the dead centre of the Peninsula and there was an imperative need to provide a thousand-seater auditorium. This was adequate for ten years during which time daughter churches were planted to help root people in their own areas. From Sunday schools the new churches built their family congregations and so a circle was spread as far as Lavender Hill, Tokai, Tableview, Atlantis, Khayelitsha, Stellenbosch, Somerset West, Ottery and Paarl.

It is an interesting fact that the growth of St James had never been conceived in expansionist terms with grandiose plans to accommodate the future. It simply seemed to happen! God was drawing up the blue print for work that was in his hands for him to work out his purposes.

1992 saw further expansion to the Sanctuary enabling it to seat 1,600; a new wing was added to the children's centre to accommodate a fully equipped creche, the larger Sunday school, Wednesday night Bible study electives and the numerous children and youth clubs meeting on Friday afternoons and evenings. Adjacent to the Sanctuary the tape ministry premises required updating to produce

1,000 tapes per month to cater for local and outside requests for sermons, Bible studies and the messages of visiting overseas speakers. A coffee shop was opened, the proceeds of which help to finance the missions fund. Adequate kitchen and toilet facilities were provided as well as a larger hall for the numerous functions and overflow from the Sanctuary. The original chapel still exists but has been refurbished to accommodate wedding ceremonies and funeral services. The large entrance foyer of the church is also utilized as a meeting place.

Music and singing, provided by trained and experienced personnel, form an integral part of worship. Various musical instruments are used as well as an effective sound system. Hymn and chorus books have been replaced by computerised screens located above the stage and controlled from a central desk. These screens are also used to highlight sermon and Bible study points as well as important notices.

In honouring God's word in Matthew 28:19 to make disciples in all the nations, a ministry referred to as 'Teach and Reach' was established similar to the 'Evangelism Explosion' programme. Its purpose is to train and encourage the individual for an evangelistic task. Training courses are run throughout the year, including clinics for pastors from other denominations. As part of its practical training, application teams of three call on homes and public shopping complexes weekly throughout the year's programme to present the gospel of Jesus Christ. We praise him for the many souls who have found salvation and who have come into a personal relationship with our Lord.

A strongly motivated and dedicated prayer group meets daily to pray for the salvation of specific people who do not know the Lord, as well as for the recovery of the sick and those perplexed with trials. This is in addition to congregational prayer meetings that meet thrice weekly.

Bible studies with fifteen electives cater for the new Christian and those seeking more advanced studies. The New and Old Testaments of the Bible as well as topical subjects of interest are included in every eight-week seminar which takes place on average 4 to 5 times a year.

Devotions and social activities cater for all ages from the tiny tot to senior adults. Creche facilities and special activities for young children allow parents to attend church services and special functions.

Church security officers help to give church attenders peace of mind. They also assist with the handling of church traffic.

Friendly and helpful ushers welcome churchgoers and help in the seating arrangements which usually cater for an ever growing overflow as well as for a large contingent of Russian visitors from visiting ships.

The provision of an efficiently run Sunday school and youth church meetings catering for 1,000 young people at the family service encourages parents to attend church, knowing their children are also enjoying the word of God in a manner appealing to their age group.

In encouraging the Christian to serve others, the Women's Ministry alone has 26 varying activities that support the work of God in the church.

The mission ministry is financially supported and upheld in prayer.

God's word is revered and adhered to above all things as we endeavour to carry out his commandments and please him with the help of his Holy Spirit.

It was indeed a dark night in the history of St James on 25 July 1993 when the church was plunged into the depths of sorrow through a massacre which is now part of our history. However, the darkness, even on that night, did not overcome the light of God as he turned such evil into good. Many people found Christ and the whole nation witnessed the way evangelical Christians respond to a crisis. To God be all the glory!

Now, what of the future? We continue to go forward, remembering that each day is a day nearer home, nearer Christ.

Ministries working towards this end, just to name a few, in addition to those already mentioned, are:

Concerned World
Counselling
Hiking Clubs
Hospital Visitation
Khayelitsha – a township for so-called 'Black' people on
  the outskirts of Cape Town
Marriage Preparation
Men's Ministry
Muslim Outreach
Prayer Ministry
Prison Ministry
Russian Ministry
Senior Adults
Teach and Reach
Women's Ministries (in excess of 23 sub-ministries)
Xhosa Bible studies

A church is only as strong as its vision.

Its vision is only as strong as its faith.

Its faith is only as strong as its closeness to the author
and finisher of its faith, the Lord Jesus Christ.

CHAPTER 17

Church Growth Through the Giving of Ourselves

REVD DR JOHN KAO

Senior Pastor of the Toronto Chinese Community Church
General Director of A.C.E.M. Canada

By the grace of our Lord Jesus Christ, we have seen his marvellous work around the world, especially among the Chinese communities in North America. Among the fast growing ministries in the Chinese churches, we have experienced his power at the Toronto Chinese Community Church. Starting with seven couples in 1975, the church has grown into five locations with eleven congregations of more than two thousand people worshipping the Lord on Sundays. The following brief report will testify to his effective work amongst his people.

For more than five years its founding pastor, Revd John Kao had travelled far and wide on behalf of Christian Nationals' Evangelism Commission and spoken in various churches for world mission. He surveyed and interviewed many fast-growing churches and collected materials to be used for church ministries. Some common elements for rapid church growth, he learnt, are expository preaching, leadership training, small-group ministry, maximum participation of lay leaders, personal evangelism, emphasis on world missions and church planting. During his trip back to Hong Kong at the end of 1974, his co-workers, under the leadership of Revd Dr Andrew Song, commissioned Revd John Kao to return to Canada for church planting ministry. Beginning with six couples, they prayed for God's guidance and prepared to pioneer gospel ministries, mostly among university students in the midtowns of Toronto.

John applied and experimented with the principles he had learned with his newly-planted church. The very first principles were expository preaching, personal evangelism, small group fellowship and giving for world missions. Even though in the first year our giving for world missions was less than one thousand Canadian dollars, we followed the good example of the Toronto People's Church in her commitment to world missions, and our annual mission fund reached nearly half a million dollars in 1994. The pastors and leaders of the church truly believe that 'it is more blessed to give than to receive'.

Disciple-making through small groups and personal involvements is one of the major emphases of our church. Scores of young people have dedicated their lives to serve the Lord. Many of them have gone through seminary training and church internship to become pastors of our various congregations.

Our church leaders have often prayed and planned together in seeking God's guidance to develop an even more effective ministry. Since 1985 we had been planning to organize the Association of Chinese Evangelical Ministries. A.C.E.M. Canada eventually was incorporated in Canada in 1989. The Lord continues to give us visions and we have therefore set our priorities in cultivating:

(1) Community of Oneness and Love,
(2) Community of Discipleship Training,
(3) Community of Church Planting and Growth,
(4) Community of World Mission, and
(5) Community of Local Concern.

These common goals and priorities have become the focuses of planning in our church ministries.

Thanks to our Lord our churches have been growing, and their vitality can be seen in the birth of new congregations, the planting of new churches and the constructing of new church buildings. New congregations have been added by language groups, moving from bilingual to uni-lingual. At present we have seven congregations in Cantonese, two congregations in Mandarin and two congregations in English. These congregations were the fruit of our church-planting ministry in new locations. The original church was set up in 1975 in Toronto; in 1979 we branched out into Scarborough; in 1987 we started a new church in Milliken; in 1990 we planted another sister church in Markham; and in 1994 we began a new mission church in North York.

The construction of new church buildings also contributes to our rapid growth. In 1981 we constructed our first building in Scarborough; in 1991 a second church building was erected in Richmond Hill; in 1994 a third church building in Milliken with the fourth one in Markham in 1995. New churches always facilitate church growth and rapid expansion of the ministries.

We look to the Lord to have ten churches planted by the year 2000 AD, with at least five thousand Christians to worship the holy name of the Lord Jesus Christ. We hope this brief testimony will glorify his name and encourage Christian co-workers to reap the harvest before our Lord's return.

CHAPTER 18

An Experiment with New Testament Principles

WILLIE O. PETERSEN, D Min

Bethel Bible Fellowship, Dallas, Texas

[Since 1965 my wife Gloria and I have been engaged in pastoral ministry. We have been on staff with Urban Evangelical Mission (UEM) since 1980. I previously served UEM as National Field Director, Vice President. My current duties include Urban Research Consultant and church planter.]

The experiences described in this brief paper reflect a pattern of what the Urban Evangelical Mission is doing nationally in many other cities. But as evangelicals, our efforts seem so small among 35 to 40 million African Americans. Our US government reports in 1990 that perhaps about a third of African Americans are not middle-class. But most of us are middle-class and ten million live in white suburban areas. But what most evangelicals in our country consider an appropriate urban ministry seems limited to a concentration on social programmes among our Black poor. And all the while a growing middle-class continues to be very responsive to a culturally relevant evangelical ministry.

In the Spring of 1989 Urban Evangelical Mission commissioned my wife Gloria and me to plant a church in an affluent section of Dallas, Texas. Our primary target audience is unchurched African American families, relocating to this community from other parts of the United States. Bethel Bible Fellowship is a congregation of approximately 100 adults in which the ministry of the church is conducted by the laymen won through outreach. These individuals are either new believers, or they personally acknowledge that for the past several years they have not been active in a church. This description fits 90% of the active adults in this new church. As for the rest, few would describe themselves as mature Christians.

A brief profile of these men and women reveals that they are African American couples earning approximately $100,000 per year. Their education ranks at least a college degree with most holding two or more professional degrees and very responsible business and professional positions. For example, both parents of the last baby to be born in our church are physicians. We dedicated that baby to the Lord in the Fall of 1993. The only marriage I performed in 1989 was that of a male doctor to a female lawyer. Yes, we have other individuals with lesser careers but these represent the norm.

It is a privilege to introduce you to some of the wonderful people the Spirit of God has touched. For example we had come to the close of the sharing time in the Sunday morning worship when a man stepped forward and asked permission to share something.

He was in his early forties and from the appearance of his clothing it was obvious that he belonged to the ranks of corporate executives.

He walked briskly down to the front and stood before an open microphone. His wife and daughters were regulars and had completed the new members' orientation class. He had occasionally visited with them.

Standing there with a wide smile across his face and a twinkle in his eyes this man spoke.

'I received Jesus Christ as my personal Saviour. Will you receive me as a member of this congregation?'

The people, many standing on their feet, broke into spontaneous applause, tears, and amens. This was the exact convincing proof the men of Bethel Bible Fellowship needed to show the women that there was a spiritual emphasis in the previous two-day men's retreat. This man was one of twenty-two men who joined the pastor and his pastoral intern for the retreat. It was held at a beautiful resort an hour away from the community of the church. There amidst golf, tennis, basketball and swimming, these African American business and professional men went to pray and to study God's word.

This testimony came after this man had been tremendously moved by the Spirit of God during the hours of discussions regarding the moral failure of King David and the subsequent grace of God. Someone pointed out that one year before, a public prayer was offered for this man's salvation at the request of his wife. Within the prayer was a specific request that one day he would stand where he stood and profess Christ, which he had just done.

The following couple clearly represent tokens of the power of God to change lives. This particular Sunday morning was special and the tears were flowing from the eyes of about half the men present. The man standing before them was saying goodbye for his family as he was taking a promotion in another city. The depth of love between these brothers could not be concealed. He was a model of success in his education and career, and had been to the best schools, the Air Force Academy, UCLA, and the University of Texas. He had easily climbed his way to the top of several major corporations. At a time when the weak economy forced many to have their careers terminated, this man was honoured with advancement. But he and his family were not happy at all – they did not wish to leave this congregation where he was now a new elder. This morning they were openly speaking of the growth and development that had occurred since they came to Bethel Bible Fellowship. Just two months before he had baptized his own seven-year-old son in the swimming pool of another elder. They recalled how their marriage had been on the verge of divorce; how they each had been guilty of selfish attitudes, but the word of God had made the difference. And this man made the most amazing of all comments.

'I anticipate that to whatever city God leads us in the future we will plant another church like Bethel Bible Fellowship in that city.'

The next two couples had all the characteristics of having everything, but they were hungry. The pastor and his wife were delighted to see that two couples were signed up for the new members orientation. Since each couple had small children it was agreed that they could each host a session in their home. The pastor and his wife arrived early and found the couples waiting. The first of the two sessions is designed to establish personal faith in Jesus Christ. The second session is to orient new people to the ministry and life of the church.

The evidences of these young African Americans' material success was everywhere. It was displayed in the beautiful neighbourhood where they lived with large houses, and in the extent to which each room was well-appointed. The very first question they were asked was for their favourite verse on which they based their salvation and this was their reply: 'We don't know a salvation verse, will you teach us one?'

The joy of that experience can be exceeded by nothing material or that money can buy. The scheduled two sessions lasted for twice the amount of time set for them. The couples were unashamed of their spiritual hunger, and they apologized for going so far beyond the normal time.

There is more to their story. After two years each couple is actively involved in the small group ministry.

Recently one of the men proudly told of this experience. He was preparing to teach a small group class how to use John 3:16 to help another person come to faith in Jesus Christ. As he rushed from his corporate meeting to his

Bible study he forgot to pick up his teaching notes. There with a large smile on his face, this successful businessman and baby Christian recounted how well he taught the material without notes as a result of his preparations.

There is more. A regular practice of Bethel Bible Fellowship is to have a pastoral intern on staff who is learning how to start up a new congregation. As one intern was about to launch a sister congregation to Bethel, a special celebration dinner was held. During that dinner the men in training to become elders for Bethel informed the pastor that they were giving the intern and his core group a cheque for $500 to encourage them in their efforts.

One thing that makes reaching the middle-class African Americans such a joy is their compassion for the poor. The ministry of an outreach group was rewarded recently when the growing group of street people to whom they ministered asked them to conduct the services every week.

For more than a year, this faithful outreach group of about twenty adults has reproduced every month the worship services of Bethel in a nearby poor community. They spend time sharing prayer requests with the home-less and street people who attend. They sing familiar songs. Both men and women tell of God's work of grace in their lives, and a laymen presents a simple short and positive Bible message on the grace of God and the power of his Spirit to change lives. Over that year they have performed many deeds of love such as giving new blankets to those living under the bridges during winter, purchasing hundreds of dollars worth of food for meals.

We are using a variety of strategies to develop a church. Networking with sister church members is our main outreach strategy. We take the position that every day there are many Christians who have contact with an unchurched person living in our target area. We identify the type of contacts we want and the specific communities they should live near. An important part of the vision we share with new believers is that we want to plant churches in the three adjoining communities. The intern pastor met with four men for nearly one year to develop a new ministry team. In the Fall of 1992 they launched the Fort Worth Bible Fellowship. We are praying that within two years the two churches will start a third one among other unchurched middle-class African Americans.

We were attracting unchurched black men through meaningful relationships and leading them from where they were to spiritual maturity. Friends provided names and addresses of unchurched friends, co-workers and relatives living in one of the target areas. Many of our mutual friends, black and white, brought their contacts to our Bible studies. Other names came from work, business, school, or social contacts. These names were followed up for as long as there was any hope of a response. We were building personal relationships with unchurched black men, for evangelism contact with them through a mutual friend. Several solid families in the church consisting of husbands, wives, and children were reached this way. The number of active families in the church may go up and then down as more mature Christians leave. Usually they leave because our philosophy of ministry allows new believers to conduct the ministry. We ask more mature Christians to support the new learners.

We use an aggressive style of social outreach which calls for speedy interactions since our population group is very mobile. We like to see them quickly get into a home for dinner, or meet for a meal in a restaurant. We are trying to place them in an appropriate and familiar environment in which we can introduce them to the vision of our church. We are teaching them these six ways to create community by:

- Promoting the Maturity of Believers
- Presenting the gospel to the Lost
- Pursuing World Missions Internationally
- Stimulating Black Family Ideals
- Affirming Black Cultural Interests
- Encouraging Inter-Racial Fellowship Among Believers

Once we establish a contact we pursue it until it bears fruit or until the man indicates in some way that we should not continue to pursue him. When a contact responds favourably to our friendship we encourage him to consider participating in one of several informal social gatherings offered by our church.

A men's breakfast is held each third Saturday in a local hotel. The setting is intended for peer interaction rather than formal Bible teaching. We take great care to select discussion topics that are related to the life situations of the men. When we conducted a survey to determine which format we should follow, the men clearly indicated that they much prefer the informal format to a Bible study format.

The average man struggles with sins of the flesh and has a deep desire to find victory over them. This creates an excellent teaching opportunity. They learn both what Scripture teaches and also how to apply it to real life.

Another great opportunity we provide for men to get together is in bi-monthly small groups. These are fellowship groups consisting of 8–12 families which meet for mutual support. This format includes a Bible study, prayer, sharing, recreation and refreshments. The Bible study is a group discussion conducted in a style in which the average person feels comfortable participating. It is our desire that the small groups will facilitate the development of meaningful relationships between individuals who do not know one another very well and that people will want to bring their unsaved friends to these groups.

Another ministry opportunity is that husbands and wives conduct these home meetings. Many seem eager to lead the Bible discussions. The women have a fellowship group similar to the men which meets on the first Saturday of each month. The women favoured a more formal organization of their structure, they seek to have more teaching and instruction than do the men. The women have certain activities that they enjoy doing, and they plan for them months ahead of time.

A large portion of the pastor's time is spent seeking to develop personal relationships with individual contacts. He works at demonstrating a genuine interest in the man and his family without making any demands on them.

Usually after a few months of association, the relationship has reached a point where the man shows some kind of interest in the church. It is not unusual that men and their wives are not Christians at the time they begin to participate in the church. Frequently it is only after an extended exposure to the gospel that they understand their need for a personal relationship to Christ. This is because, even if they have a religious background, most have little biblical training.

I find among the men I follow-up a significant number have personal struggles which we share together as friends. I listen and I try to show compassion. I pray for wisdom as I gently guide them toward biblical solutions. But I always leave it to them to make their own choices with no threat of undoing our friendship if they make a wrong choice. The personal struggles generally range from alcohol and drug addictions, to troubled finances and the consequences of adultery and other marital conflicts. Several have expressed regret for the damage they have done to their marriages. For some there is a previous divorce and remarriage in their background; for some even two previous divorces. When their present marriage seems to be in trouble they are very concerned and want help. But for each one that opens up and honestly shares, many more for various reasons acknowledge no need for help.

Once a man makes the transition from a ministry observer to participant in the ministry we provide opportunities for him to develop. The church and its various ministries have a very simple design to encourage those with minimum experience, knowledge, or skills to take charge of a ministry. The objective is that while the babe gains biblical content, he also develops practical ministry experience. One should be able to apply what is being taught from the Scriptures.

As a result of this type of system, believers with limited abilities operate the total ministry of this church. There are four basic ministry areas, and all activity falls within the area of one of these four categories:

- Fellowship
- Leadership
- Teaching
- Worship.

One sentence descriptions are used to describe a list of twenty-five ministry opportunities. The inquirer is able to make additional suggestions if he so desires.

Allowing the laymen quickly to assume leadership roles in the new church has many advantages. For example, it is much easier for laymen to recruit laymen for ministry than it is for me as the professional. A layman can much more easily identify with a layman than with a professional. As laymen are engaged in doing ministry they discover new and better ways of doing things, thus the quality of the ministry is improved. The system of quickly enlisting laymen to operate a ministry leads to a sense of ownership and a proper pride in the work because most of the ministry will be developed by them. These and various other advantages I have observed as a result of this approach to the ministry.

I give most of my attention to leadership training. I act as a coach to those who accept responsibilities to ensure them success in what they are doing. When the ministry first began it was necessary for me to take a new individual and help him select a ministry, but now it is being done in two basic ways:

(1) teams will recruit a person to work with their group, or,
(2) men who have watched me work with a new person now follow my example. They seek out uninvolved individuals and help them to find a suitable ministry.

God has been slowly adding families to the ministry and we have a core of about forty families. These people are the primary leaders, they direct all the ministries of the church. My role continues to be leadership training and support. The church provides its own financial resources for the ministry. Each week 20% is set aside for missions and saving. In addition to supporting church planting in the USA, the church shares a mission tithe with several Third World missions leaders around the world. The small group ministry includes prayer and correspondence with two assigned missionaries for each group.

CHAPTER 19

Rolling Hills Covenant Church, California

PASTOR JAMES C. CREASMAN

HISTORY AND ORGANIZATION

Rolling Hills Covenant Church was started on Palm Sunday, April 14, 1957, with 52 charter members meeting in a local school. The Community Church of San Pedro and a Torrance home group joined together as founders of the new church. Today, the church is located 20 miles south of Los Angeles on 7.25 acres and has a membership in excess of 2,200 people.

In 1964, the first missionaries were sent out by the young church. John and Lou Lungren, former youth pastor and his wife, were sent to Honduras and a former church chairman, Dr Paul Carlson, and his wife Lois were sent to the Belgian Congo. Dr Carlson had had a vision of becoming a medical missionary in his student days and diligently worked toward that goal. Lois had trained as a nurse and joined Dr Carlson with their two young children. His tragic death at the hands of the rebels during the Congolese uprising in 1964 caused national concern for the unsung heroes and heroines out in the mission fields. It also caused the Rolling Hills Covenant Church body to remain strongly dedicated to the Great Commission of Jesus Christ.

Since that time, the church has grown to a large, strong influence in the area. In 1985 our first full-time Missions Pastor, James Creaseman, was hired. He has encouraged members of the congregation to become personally involved in mission fields. In the later part of the 1980s the structure of the church organization changed to the Elder system and Commissions covering the various phases of church life. Members of the Commissions are elected by the congregation. The Missions Commission consists of an elder, eight diaconate, the missions pastor and the church chairman and senior pastor as ex-officio members.

In 1989 a comprehensive Missions Handbook was published to conform to church by-laws. As stated in the handbook, 'Rolling Hills Covenant Church exists to glorify God by demonstrating his attributes and character to the world through both our individual lives and our corporate life as a church, in obedience to Christ's commands as contained in the holy Scriptures concerning the evangelization and discipleship of all peoples.

This requires that we be responsible, maturing, and reproducing disciples who understand the Spirit-filled life and who walk daily in the lordship of Jesus Christ, building solid Christian lives and homes based on God's word, and that we seek to persuade others within our community and around the world to place their faith in the Lord Jesus Christ and become responsible members of his church.

Rolling Hills Covenant Church places a high priority on the evangelization and discipleship of all nations. We believe God desires the local church to be the primary means for sending people to proclaim the saving message of Jesus Christ to wherever people inhabit the earth.

The role of the church in this great world-wide venture is to confirm those whom God is calling, help to equip them effectively for life and ministry, and send them out with sufficient resources and encouragement for their vital task.'

The scriptural purposes of our involvement in missions are to glorify God (1 Cor. 10:13), to fulfil the Great Commission of Christ (Mt. 28:19–20), to share Christ's heart for the world (Mt. 9:36–38; 18:10–14), to see men saved and brought to the knowledge of God (Jn. 3:16, Acts 1:8, Rom. 10:13–15), to build up the body of Christ through discipling (Eph. 4:11–16) and to minister to the totality of human need (Mt. 22:37–39; 25:31–46). We believe that the Bible teaches that many methods and means can be used to reach the world with the gospel of Jesus Christ. Such practices would include Bible trans-lation, schools to train national leaders, multimedia ministries (radio, TV, films, etc.), medical and relief work, building and maintenance of mission facilities and equip-ment, school teaching for missionary children, business administration and secretarial needs and writing, printing and distribution of literature.

We define missions as 'the sending out of specifically equipped disciple-makers who cross barriers of distance, culture, or language in order to establish and strengthen the church in places beyond the normal sphere of influence of our members'.

Mission, then, is specifically cross-cultural outreach, whereas evangelism includes sharing the gospel in one's own culture. Mission is defined primarily by culture, rather than by geography. The allocation of the missions budget covers the following categories with emphasis in the following order of priority:

a. Outreach 3 – Unreached cross-cultural.
    This would include missionaries working in people groups where the predominant religion is one other than Christian.
b. Outreach 2 – Reached cross-cultural.
    This area of outreach would include work with other cultural groups both within and outside of the United

States. This would include missionaries working in people groups where there is an established church.

c. Outreach 1 – Homocultural Ministries.
   Ministries within the culture of Rolling Hills Covenant Church which carry on a work that is not the normal responsibility of a local church.

d. Outreach 0 – Ministries not connected with the actual support of missionaries or mission organizations.
   This includes conference and retreat expenses, mission commission expenses, short-term missions and field expenses.

Direct financial support from our missions budget may be up to one-third of the annual support needs of the full-time missionary. A higher percentage may be allocated for missionaries from our congregation; the recommended maximum would be 50% for such individuals. Support for short-term service is up to one-half of all expenses, excluding summer missionaries. Summer missionaries are supported up to one third of all expenses, not to exceed $1,000.

PRACTICAL APPLICATIONS

Education of the Congregation

A continuing educational tool used by the Missions Education Ministry Team has been an annual Missions awareness week. Such themes as 'Where in the World are You God?' 'To the Ends of the Earth' and 'Make Disciples of All Nations' have been used. Guest speakers are invited to speak at special meetings, Sunday morning services and panel discussions. Some years a fair has been planned that emphasizes international food booths, films, musical concerts and activities to involve adults and children of all ages in missionary awareness.

An on-going 'Adopt a Missionary' programme began in 1982. This was initiated to have each Sunday school class adopt a missionary by writing letters and learning about the family. This has also evolved into a small group that meets Sunday morning to pray specifically for the ministries of the Church, outreach to the South Bay community and for churches to be established among the unreached peoples of the world.

For the past several years Rolling Hills Covenant has ended the year by holding the 'Bethlehem Bazaar'. The bazaar is an alternative gift market that allows 'shoppers' to choose interesting gifts such as ox carts, donkeys and seed on behalf of a loved one as a Christmas gift. Gift cards are provided to send to the recipient to announce what was purchased and thank them.

In 1987, a church member brought to our church a course on 'Perspectives on the World Christian Movement'. This course involves sixteen meetings and is open to members of neighbouring churches as well as Rolling Hills Covenant members. This is an on-going ministry that has grown each year. Additionally, a church member has begun publishing a monthly prayer list called FRONTLINES that highlights a local outreach ministry or Rolling Hills Covenant Church overseas ministry activity for daily prayer. This is included in the Worship Folder for the Saturday evening and Sunday morning services and reaches the entire congregation. In addition, we produce a brochure listing over 55 world-wide missionaries and their families for whom we contribute support. Each missionary family submits specific needs and prayer requests.

Recruitment and Training

The Recruitment and Training Ministry Team was organized to channel all interested missions candidates into training and counselling to better equip them to attain their goals. The committee developed book lists, agency information, career and education requirement information as well as a continuing discipleship programme. The committee then focused on developing potential missionaries and selectively taking on new missionaries. A formal programme for training potential missionaries from within the congregation entitled 'World Christian Preparation Process' was developed. It is the desire of the Missions Commission, under the direction of the Missions Pastor and the Council of Elders, to help nurture and develop members of the congregation whom God may be calling to missionary work. The process provides the basic framework around which the church and the individual, working together in an interdependent partnership, can arrive at a mutually agreed upon course of action for discerning God's calling and timing for cross-cultural ministry.

The purposes of the preparation process are to assist the individual in his growth as he conforms to the image of Jesus Christ and to assist in developing a 'World Christian' lifestyle. This preparation involves four stages.

Stage I, Exposure (World Christian) Requires

1. Attend church and Sunday School regularly.
2. Become a church member and be baptized.
3. Attend the World Christian Forum.
4. Develop a friendship with at least one missionary.
5. Attend missions conferences.
6. Experience one or more short-term missions or participate in RHCC cross-cultural ministries.
7. Meet with the missions pastor.
8. Read the Stage I book list.

Stage II, Preparation (Potential Missionary)

1 Continue programmes suggested in stage one.
2 Meet regularly with a World Christian Discipleship Group.
3. Attend the 'Perspectives on the World Christian Movement' course.
4. Pursue any required formal education.
5. Semi-annually present a report to the missions pastor.
6. Read the Stage II book list.

Stage III, Decision (Missionary Candidate)

1. Meet with the Recruitment and Training Ministry Team.
2. Choose and apply to an agency.
3. Prepare a study paper on the anticipated country of service.
4. Meet with the missions pastor as needed.
5. Read the Stage III books.

Stage IV, Departure (Missionary Internship)

1. Develop a support team.
2. Be commissioned.
3. Pack. Go!

Summer missions have been used for several years to give people training and exposure to mission work. In 1986, 25 dedicated people were sent out from the church. In 1993, Rolling Hills Covenant Church had its most fruitful year ever by sending out 120 people to 18 locations including the choir team to Eastern Europe, a college team to Trinidad, a high school team to Jamaica, a singles team to Moscow and families to the Navajos in Arizona.

Cross Cultural – Community

A ministry team was formed to minister to a core-group of approximately 25 Hispanic people. The first year 10 to 15 made first-time decisions for Christ. Over the years this group has evolved into the Hispanic Church at Rolling Hills Covenant, pastored by Gwynn Lewis, a former church missionary. In December of 1990, they sent their first missionary to Central America. The church has grown to over 100 attendees. It has been involved in the planting of another Hispanic congregation at the Orange Covenant Church; has sent a church planter to the Oakland, California area, and sponsored two short-term missionaries to Guatemala.

Thirty-six tutors taught English to approximately 300

speakers of other languages from nine nations at our Laubach centre. Eight college students have provided summer day camps for ninety-five Harbor Hills public housing children. The Filipino Congregation worshipping at Rolling Hills Covenant Church has continued to grow and now has over 75 attendees. They called Pastor Pabalate from the Philippines as their senior pastor.

'Feed My Sheep' is a ministry developed in 1989 to help meet the physical as well as the spiritual needs of those who are temporarily or permanently unable to care for themselves. The ministry has had a very active role supporting local poor Hispanic families through food distribution, as well as supporting two local drug rehabilitation centres and two groups within the church who are ministering to the homeless.

Through the devastation of the 1992 riots in Los Angeles, Rolling Hills Covenant Church became very close to the Compton Covenant Church located in the affected area. A group of Rolling Hills men have, for the past two years, supplied 80 to 100 bags of groceries each week to the residents of this area. Additionally, funding and moral support has been given by the Rolling Hills congregation to assist in the continuing ministry of the Compton church.

MAXIMIZING THE MOMENT 1993–1994

Objective

The Missions Commission has selected the country of Kazakhstan in the former Soviet Union on which to focus our ministry efforts in a multidimensional plan involving both short and long-term missions. The Commission believes God has led our congregation to a strategic involvement in Kazakhstan through our philosophy of missions emphasizing church planting among unreached peoples, through the giftedness and calling of people in our church who have overwhelmingly responded to the needs of the Kazakh people, and through unprecedented responsiveness to the gospel in this Central Asian country.

Of the ten million Kazakhs in the world, seven million are in Kazakhstan. When the first team of five summer missionaries from the Career class went to Kazakhstan in 1991, there were only 20 known Kazakh Christians. The majority of Kazakhs are Muslim, and some atheist. Two years later, after another summer team that helped plant the first Kazakh church, and Rolling Hills Covenant Church members hosting a group of Kazakhs in homes here, and sending our first long-term missionary to Kazakhstan, there are now two Kazakh churches and about 300 Kazakh Christians.

In the summer of 1993 a College/Career Team of twelve, a family of five, and a Vision Team of twelve was sent to Kazakhstan. Currently there is a long-term resident missionary in place and there are several other people either considering or preparing for long-term mission service. There is a team of people known as Prayer Team 2000 meeting twice a month to join the intercessory prayer for the Kazakhs. There is also a leadership team emerging to research, plan and mobilize the congregation in an effort to reach Kazakhs for Christ. Adopting the Kazakh people is a further step in our missions commitment. That commitment has been marked by several distinctives:

1) Primacy of unreached peoples – endeavouring to be strategic in its missions participation, targeting people groups where the Church has not yet been established.
2) Support of indigenous workers – endeavouring to be effective in its missions participation, by using financial resources to support mature and gifted believers from the target population who don't need the extensive support structure and cross-cultural adjustment of missionaries who are coming from outside the culture.
3) Promotion of short-term missions – endeavouring to

be relevant in its missions participation, involving the whole body at Rolling Hills Covenant Church through exposing as many people as possible to firsthand cross-cultural ministry, and by providing contact between the congregation and those who have gone on a mission.

4) Participation with the whole Body of Christ – endeavouring to be co-operative in its missions participation, realizing that the world cannot be reached for Christ without recognizing that God's desire is for his Body to be united, Rolling Hills Covenant Church consistently works through missions agencies and partners with churches and believers in missions efforts.

5) Consistency with the missions philosophy – the adoption of the Kazakh people is probably the most strategic missions effort ever undertaken by the RHCC. The Kazakh people, with no known church and only a handful of Christians among 10 million just two years ago, qualify as one of the world's most unreached and unevangelized peoples.

Methods and Means

In order to mobilize the entire congregation to participate in outreach to the Kazakhs it would mean finding ways of making it relevant to all aspects of the ministry, such as:

- Empowering the Kazakh Task Force and the supervision of the Missions Commission and Missions Pastor to mobilize the congregation to reach the Kazakhs.
- Endorsing the Prayer Team 2000 emphasis on prayer for the Kazakhs, including a month of fasting and prayer and regular inclusion in worship service prayer time throughout the year.
- Supporting on-going communication with the congregation on the status of Kazakh outreach through regular worship folder inserts, posters, and verbal and multimedia presentations in classes, small groups, and worship services.

- Giving a substantial one-time contribution to establish an initial working relationship.

CONCLUSION

Throughout its history, Rolling Hills Covenant Church has been marked by a commitment to missions. Fulfilling the Great Commission has not been an optional part of our identity, it has always been central to who we are and what we are about. We have consistently made it a top priority in our preaching, teaching, praying, giving and serving. By adopting the Kazakhs, we are expressing the same commitment by taking on a more focused all-church emphasis. May God help us to continue to be faithful in the gospel, within our buildings and homes, throughout our community and around the world.

CHAPTER 20

Elmbrook Church, Waukesha, Wisconsin

DR D. STUART BRISCOE

WHO WE ARE

Elmbrook Church is a non-denominational church located in Waukesha, Wisconsin, a western suburb of Milwaukee. The church began in 1957 with five families and has grown into a 3,000 member church serving over 6,000 worshippers on a given weekend. As the church has grown, each of Elmbrook's sub-ministries has developed and they are now overseen by 21 associate pastors. Through each of these ministries, Elmbrook focuses on making an impact on its members, community, and world. Described below are several of our ministries' goals and accounts of what God is doing through them.

CHILDREN'S MINISTRIES

It's a familiar scenario, men and women leave home and leave their religious roots behind. They get married and have their first child and find themselves looking for some moral and spiritual stability for their children. It is a common occurrence to find many of these new parents drifting into Elmbrook's doors.

The Children's Ministry uses this opportunity to encourage the parents to be concerned about their baby's growth and also confronts them with the question of their own relationship with God. Classes are offered for first-time parents, teaching them about Christianity and showing them that they can be used by God to teach their children. Once this is understood, Elmbrook provides the opportunity for informed and committed parents to dedicate their children to the Lord, vowing to teach them (through word and example) how to live as believers.

An infant who grows through Elmbrook's children's ministries will have numerous programmes to get involved in. The ministries are age-graded and provide nursery, Sunday school, and mid-week clubs for over 2,000 children. Each Sunday-school class is assigned one of Elmbrook's missionaries. They correspond with their missionary, learn about the country where their missionary lives and works and give their Sunday school offering specifically to the missionary's ministry. Another effective community outreach includes a licensed day-care centre called Elmbrook Church Child Enrichment Centre (ECCEC) that works daily with 300 children. Summer neighbourhood Bible clubs are held in sponsors' homes and volunteers are encouraged to keep in touch with the children and their families in their neighbourhood for service and outreach.

Approximately 1,000 are needed to staff the children's ministry [parents, volunteers, and student assistants]. Leaders admit that recruiting for positions is difficult but emphasize that they are offering people a gift – an opportunity to serve the Lord that will be rewarded, both in this life, and the next.

STUDENT MINISTRIES: JUNIOR HIGH, SENIOR HIGH, COLLEGE-AGE

After students move on to Junior High and forward, they begin to grapple with the tough questions in their lives and consider what it means to take ownership of their Christian faith. The student ministries at Elmbrook seek to equip students with scriptural truth and provide more opportunities to live out the faith they profess.

The Junior High ministry is structured in a way that ministers to 6–8th graders' 'head, heart, and hands'. They minister to the 'head' stating that 'Christian faith roots not in our own thoughts but in God's revelation of himself in Jesus Christ'. Through Sunday school, students walk through a survey of the Bible, and are taught about their relationship with God.

They minister to the 'heart'. 'Christian faith means that God not only teaches us but inwardly transforms us.' Through mid-week evening meetings, GodSquad meets and examines real-life issues and what God has to say about them. Junior Highers are shown that we love God not because we have to, but because we want to.

They stress the importance of 'hands' in that 'Christian faith doesn't stay in our heads and hearts but moves out in actions'. Through the King's Kids drama team, Crossroads choir, teaching assistant opportunities, summer work camps, and RadioHeads – an amateur radio club that supports overseas missionaries – Junior Highers have an opportunity to serve in significant ways.

Senior High incorporates large group meetings (Insight) and small groups (Outtasight) that alternate weekly. Through the Insight meetings students have the opportunity to hear speakers address timely issues affecting their everyday lives. Outtasight incorporates small group dynamics that emphasize fellowship, discipleship, and accountability. Both programmes provide opportunities for outreach.

Senior High students also have opportunities in the summer to serve on a short-term missions trip, participate in Work Camp, or serve at the Children's Ministry Kid's Kamp. Each programme is designed for students to serve the Lord in a cross-cultural context. A cross-cultural ministry may be experienced by going overseas, serving at a rescue mission downtown, or serving children through Kid's Kamp. This ministry has a solid base of dedicated adult leadership and a strong core of students who take their faith seriously. Students On Another Road (SOAR) is made up of many key students who meet every other week to pray for their schools, families, friends, and each other.

College-Age stresses the importance of reaching the world for Christ by participating in short-term missions, Urbana, and reaching out to their colleges or work places. As students begin to make life choices as to what they want to do with their lives, Elmbrook's College-Age encourages students to think about how they will serve the Lord, whatever the vocation.

ADULT CHRISTIAN EDUCATION

Adult education at Elmbrook ranges from introductory classes to masters level extension classes through Trinity Evangelical Divinity School (TEDS). The Evangelism and Discipleship Ministry and the Study Centre spearhead these classes.

There is a three-fold approach to evangelism. First, to equip and prepare people for the work of evangelism. This is done through Sunday classes on 'How to Give Away Your Faith' and through retreats that are held throughout the year. Second, the actual work of evangelism. Courses like 'Christianity 101' and 'Run Through the Bible' offer an appropriate environment for people who are exploring Christianity and are looking for answers. Third, we host large evangelistic events. Executive dinners for business men, British Tea luncheons for women, and family events provide opportunities for people to have an enjoyable time and hear talks on relevant topics. Large group events provide vehicles for believers to bring their friends and introduce them to the gospel.

The discipleship programme has four dimensions. First, there is one-on-one discipleship. Second, there is the discipleship class, where 40–50 new believers are instructed in a small group setting for 10 weeks. Third, there is a training class to teach people how to disciple others. Fourth, the Evangelism and Discipleship Ministry serves as a resource to all the other Elmbrook ministries. Great care is taken to ensure that Elmbrook's evangelism and discipleship programmes are relevant and available for those seeking to understand Christianity and grow as disciples.

Elmbrook's Study Centre provides Masters level classes through the Trinity Evangelical Divinity School extension programme. Through the Study Centre, students may complete the Masters of Arts in Religion degree. Many have taken advantage of the convenient location and the reasonable tuition (classes cost one-third less than a course at TEDS). Averaging 160 students per quarter, half the students are non-Elmbrook members and a third are minorities. Through this ministry, Elmbrook hopes to serve Metro-Milwaukee churches by equipping their leaders and to serve our own lay people by training them for more effective service in the body.

MEN'S MINISTRY

The desire of the Men's Ministry is for men to be solid in their beliefs and disciplines, to be equipped to use their spiritual gifts for service, and to be sent out to make a difference in their home community, workplace, and the world. Two key areas through which the Men's Ministry is realizing these goals is the Top Gun programme and Man to Missions. Top Gun is a discipleship training programme that equips men in the disciplines of the faith while providing accountability. Men meet in groups of twelve to study, pray, and spur one another on to live out the faith that they profess. Top Gun is in its second year and has 96 men involved with 16 leaders.

Top Gun's impact is being felt beyond the men's ministry. As men become leaders, they are beginning to make contributions to other Elmbrook ministries and in the home. Some of the most favourable responses come from women who have seen the change in their husband's lives. Further, Top Gun has turned into the Men's Ministry prototype for churches around the state and country to follow and use. Videos and representatives are being used to inform and teach other churches about our Top Gun material. Top Gun plans to have a special booth at the Promise Keeper men's conference this year as well.

Another key area, Man to Missions, has been in existence for 15 years. In the past, this ministry has been devoted to sending men overseas for construction-oriented projects. These projects are now being expanded and provide more opportunities for men to use their athletic, medical, business, and construction skills to minister overseas. These trips are called 'Vision Trips' or 'Vacations With a Purpose' because they are not so much mission trips as opportunities for men to be changed and exposed to their world.

Each Man to Missions team takes a ten-week course preparing them for service. The trip lasts one to two weeks and is viewed not as the end, but the beginning of a greater understanding of missions and is a stepping stone for greater involvement in the Elmbrook missions pro-gramme whether that is through supporting missionaries or exploring a deeper missionary commitment.

Currently, one of the most exciting projects is in Romania where businessmen are working to help the local people to develop a second-hand clothes store that will use its profits to support a full-time pastor and save money for their own church building.

WOMEN'S MINISTRIES

Elmbrook's Women's Ministries strives to reach out to single and married women through programmes and Bible studies that meet mornings and evenings. Morning Break, Moms'N'More, and Evening Edition incorporate large group meetings where speakers address particular topics and small groups where women stay in the same small group for a year for instruction and accountability. The women's ministry serves over 800 women in these programmes providing ministry opportunities for the homemaker and the professional.

Like the Men's Ministry, the Women's Ministry is incorporating programmes like 'Vacations With a Purpose'. This year they plan to link women with other Elmbrook women missionaries in Mexico City, Colorado Valley, Venezuela, and Caracas, Venezuela to provide them with missionary experiences from a women's perspective. Experiences like these are aimed at helping women to understand what female missionaries go through and how to support and pray specifically for our women missionaries.

SMALL GROUP MINISTRY

Twenty years ago, Elmbrook decided to drop its mid-week service and encourage people to get involved with a small group in their neighbourhood. Since its inception, small groups have grown to blanket Metro-Milwaukee with over 60 Neighbourhood Groups and Couples groups. These groups continue to serve Elmbrook by providing opportunities for people to have close fellowship in a very large church. Further, Elmbrook's experiences with small groups have allowed us to serve other churches by providing seminars for building a small group ministry. Four principles govern our small groups. Each group must grow in Bible Study, Worship, Fellowship, and Evangelism/Service. Through these guide-lines, people minister and are ministered to, learn to use their spiritual gifts, and make an impact in their neighbourhoods.

The small group ministry also serves as a base of support for prayer and encouragement for overseas missionaries. Each group has a missionary assigned to it. This provides opportunities for small groups to have a global perspective and gives missionaries specific ties to Elmbrook.

COUNSELLING MINISTRY

Elmbrook's Counselling Ministry, one of the nation's largest church-based recovery programmes, has over ten active recovery support groups, a lay counselling centre, and on-going supervision and training seminars. Through this ministry they are able to minister to people with emotional and psychological needs in a Christian context.

The Counselling Ministry has around sixty lay counsellors and trainees who do personal counselling and lead support groups. Becoming a member of the lay counselling staff takes devotion. Each prospective counsellor must be interviewed, have a recommendation from the staff, take the Minnesota Multiphasic Personality Inventory (MMPI), and complete a pastoral counselling course through the Trinity Evangelical Divinity School extension programme. Further, each lay counsellor meets with a professional supervisor weekly. Elmbrook's Counselling Ministry provides a needed outreach to hurting people and direction that points them to the good news of the gospel.

URBAN AND SOCIAL CONCERNS MINISTRY

Elmbrook's Urban and Social Concerns Ministry approaches evangelism through addressing social and spiritual needs. Both are important and are needed to present the gospel of Jesus Christ to hurting people. As a result, the Urban and Social Concerns Ministry takes steps to meet people's physical needs through tangible means and spiritual needs though proclaiming the gospel. These include:

- Ministering to 12 penal institutions in the state. This is done through music, preaching, and sports.
- Supporting crisis pregnancy centres through financial support and volunteer counsellors.
- Working with the tutoring programmes, friendship building, vacation Bible schools, and day-care centres with the Milwaukee Rescue Mission.

- Christian Employment Network Service where, with the help of three other inner-city churches, a programme is being set up to work with companies and the unemployed to help people find jobs.

One of the biggest efforts of this ministry is in its involvement with the Christian Partnership for Urban Action (CPUA). CPUA consists of 13 churches (six black, six white, 1 Asian) and its goal is to show to a watching world that multi-cultural churches can work and minister together in mutual love and respect.

CPUA sponsors numerous services and conferences promoting corporate worship and understanding and ministry outreaches such as Operation Jericho. Operation Jericho consists of inner-city and suburban churches working together to start Bible studies in one of the most dangerous parts of Milwaukee. Residents are approached by volunteers (one white and one black) to host a Bible study in their home. Sixty homes have responded to the invitation.

Other goals of CPUA are to start Time Out programmes in the Milwaukee Public Schools and to implement a dental clinic at the Milwaukee rescue mission to help the working poor. Projects such as these reach out to the community and promote relationship building among the churches.

FINE ARTS MINISTRY

John Wesley said, 'Preach as often as possible and use words when necessary.' The Fine Arts ministry at Elmbrook proclaims the good news using the arts as a way to reach out and inspire. In a Sunday service, an attendee may witness choral, classical, blue-grass, contemporary, and/or classical music. In addition, drama and dance are incorporated occasionally. The emphasis of unity within diversity and diversity within unity allows for many forms of art to be used in leading people to worship the Lord. Beyond Sundays, special drama, choir, and instrumental groups minister to prisons, hospitals, and inner-city churches. Instruments are also provided for missionary children who desire to learn music and are in need. Elmbrook's Centre for the Arts provides fine arts instruction for children and adults in music, art, cooking, and ballet. Students receive instruction from people who are both growing Christians and good artists. Through the testimony of our 15 fine arts teachers, 250 students are trained and influenced by their expertise and witness. The Fine Arts Ministry predicts that this outreach will grow to 500–600 students in the next few years.

Elmbrook's new Worship Centre was dedicated in February and provides numerous opportunities for outreach through musical dramas at Christmas and Easter. Further, Elmbrook hopes to serve the community by providing the new centre for city orchestras and special concerts.

MEDIA MINISTRY

Elmbrook's Media Ministry – Telling the Truth (TTT) grew from an improvised procedure where tape machines were wired together and duplicated in a member's mobile home to a far-reaching ministry that broadcasts out of 15 stations in the US and reaches the world. Due to the availability of Christian programming in the US, Elmbrook has concentrated its radio broadcasting efforts overseas.

TTT broadcasts to Europe, Far East, Australia, Caribbean, Africa, South America. Elmbrook serves missionaries through the TTT tape ministry by providing tapes of all the Sunday services for them. Missionaries have told countless stories of how the tapes have encouraged them or have made an impact on others who have listened to them.

'In Reality' and 'Bridges' has expanded the Media Ministry into television. 'In Reality' is currently being broadcast on a local network station weekly and is making the biggest thrust into the community. Over 25,000 see 'In Reality' in one day. 'Bridges', featuring Jill Briscoe, currently broadcasts on a Christian network and has plans in the future to broadcast on a local network.

MISSIONS

On the average, 25% of Elmbrook's budget has been allocated to missions. Currently, Missions supports 125 missionaries, works with 8 organizations, and contributes to 45 institutional agencies that reach out to more than 40 countries.

Due to Elmbrook's emphasis on missions and the increase of members that were being sent off as missionaries, guide-lines were instituted in 1981 in order to keep the Missions Ministry focused. Since then, Elmbrook has supported only missionaries who were members (prior non-members were grandfathered). This has allowed Elmbrook to give more support and attention to our own missionaries and has been helpful in establishing itself as a home church for missionaries.

Further, the missions committee has determined that 80% of its missions budget will go toward missionaries who are reaching unreached people groups.

Currently, 70 of our 125 missionaries are members of Elmbrook, and we send out 6–8 new missionary units each year. Along with financial support, missionaries receive training and encouragement. Each unit has worked with Val Hayworth, Associate Pastor of Missions, for approximately 5–6 years in preparation for their service. Once the missionary unit is sent out, they are paired up with one of our small groups who pray and write letters to them.

On furlough, missionaries have an opportunity to be served by and to serve the church by reporting to the missions committee and sharing about their work to the congregation, small group, Sunday school, and/or ministry event. This is a time that strengthens the ties between Elmbrook and its missionaries.

Elmbrook's commitment to missions is clearly seen in the priority that is given to our annual missions week where missionaries are given a very high profile and are encouraged to share with the congregation about their ministry work. During this week, we have a special keynote speaker and all other ministries focus on making missions a priority for the week.

Our Faith Promise is our annual financial commitment that each member pledges to give toward missions for the following year. Thanks to the discipline and commitment of our members, contributions are usually in excess of 100% of the $1.5 million Faith Promise Budget.

CONCLUDING REMARKS

Although Elmbrook's ministries are specialized, all work together to provide a consistent, united proclamation of the gospel of Jesus Christ. Practically, the pastoral staff meets together every Monday morning for study, prayer, and business which serves as a valuable time of information sharing, trouble shooting, and encouragement.

The goal of this church is ultimately to make disciples of all nations and to encourage all members to make an impact in their world. Stuart Briscoe recently offered the following as the battle cry of Elmbrook Church:

> We the people of God, in order to form a more realistic community of believers; establish righteousness; ensure values that will promote orderly living in marriages, home and families, encourage the spiritual and practical well-being of those living in the sphere of our influence; and secure the blessing of the liberty from selfishness and sinfulness which only the Spirit of God can provide both for ourselves and for our precious children and grandchildren; commit ourselves to our Lord and his Church to be what we were created and redeemed to be.

We thank the Lord for what he has done through Elmbrook Church and what he will continue to do locally and globally as we obediently submit to him.

CHAPTER 21

The Story of the International Assembly, New York

T. E. KOSHY

(The people referred to in this article are real, but their identities are withheld for obvious reasons.)

INTRODUCTION AND THE BEGINNING OF THE CHURCH

Churches have been sending out missionaries from their midst since the days of Paul and Barnabas. There have probably been few instances in church history, however, of a missionary outreach like the one taking place through a congregation in the University area.

Unlike other churches, when the International Assembly sends out missionaries, they are usually nationals of the country to which they are going. International Assembly, a fellowship that reaches out and ministers to foreign students at Syracuse University, now has former members bearing witness for Christ in their homelands on all major continents and in more than 20 countries throughout the world.

Today the Assembly, a non-denominational local church that has been referred to by James H Doupe in Salt Shaker — a local Christian publication — as the 'United

Nations for Christ' consists of believers from 15 to 20 countries, both Americans and foreigners, students and non-students.

International Assembly was the result of my evangelistic work among international students at Syracuse University. Syracuse, New York USA. It began as a house church in 1969.

I arrived in Syracuse, New York, in the fall of 1965 to do my graduate work in journalism at Syracuse University. During the 1960s America was going through a cultural revolution. The modern post-Christian America was born in the 1960s. It was a time of youth rebellion against any authority and values – biblical or traditional. They filled the vacuum with drugs, rock music and ungodliness. International students and scholars who came to America thinking it was a Christian country were caught in the cross-fire of this cultural 'me-generation'. Many internationals felt they had come to the wrong place and began looking for answers to life and friends to turn to.

During that time, while I was praying and wondering why I had come to this country, the Lord spoke to me and directed me to befriend and minister to internationals who were looking for a friend to turn to. I said to the Lord that many of these internationals were non-Christian intellectuals and that they did not care for him and, moreover, they were hard to convert. The Lord replied saying, 'Koshy I love them and I died for them. They are lonely – they are looking for a friend to turn to. I have no feet to go to them. I have no hand to touch them. Won't you be my feet and my hands to minister to their needs. I don't want you to convert anyone. You do the loving, caring and serving and I will do the converting. I love and care for them all regardless of whether they care for me or not.' Reluctantly I said 'Yes' to the Lord. When I said that, my heart was filled with the love of God for people of all nations regardless of colour, creed and culture. The love of God began constraining me to serve others in love. Thus began the Friendship Evangelism at Syracuse

University, and it impacted other campuses across the USA and Canada.

I knew the way to the hearts of people was through their stomachs. I began inviting students to my apartment for meals and fellowship. Many of these students were moved by the love and friendship. As I began to 'scratch where it itches', many began to ask me the reason for my love and service. My answer was, 'because there is a God who loves and cares for you. He directed me to do this for you.' Eventually a weekly Bible class started. The Lord began drawing people to himself.

Then in 1969 Brother Bakht Singh came to visit us in Syracuse. When he saw the ministry among internationals he asked me what I was doing with the new converts. I told him I sent them to local churches. But, unfortunately, many of these students were not growing in the Lord as most local churches were not catering to the spiritual needs of these international Christians. Many of these students were turned off by the lack of love they experienced in these churches. Therefore, Brother Bakht Singh (who himself was a foreign student and was converted to Christ while studying in Canada) advised me that as evangelists, our responsibility is not only to see that the souls are saved, but also to plant living churches where they can be discipled and nurtured in the Lord. He challenged me to start a 'home church' primarily to cater for the new converts. Thus began the first meeting in our home as a local church in the year 1969, about 25 years ago.

THE PATTERN OF THE CHURCH

From the beginning we wanted the International Assembly to be a local church with a difference – a missionary out-reach church patterned after the church at Antioch.

When we study the church at Antioch we see 11 principles which are biblical and transferable to the present time, place and culture. As we see in Acts chapters 11–13 the church at Antioch was:

(1) A local church with a global view – a church which consisted of world-class Christians.
(2) It was a multicultural church.
(3) It had plurality of leadership.
(4) Its leadership consisted of people of various backgrounds – racial, ethnic, cultural.
(5) It was a church which did everything with one accord in mind and purpose.
(6) It was a church that was led by the Holy Spirit.
(7) It was a worshipping church – practising corporate worship.
(8) It was a church that demonstrated the love of God in a practical way.
(9) It was a caring church.
(10) It was a missionary church that sent out mighty missionaries like Paul and Barnabas.
(11) It was a praying and fasting church which continuously sought and did the will of God.

As a result, God used the church at Antioch to evangelize and plant churches through the apostle Paul, Barnabas and other early Christian missionaries in the then known world.

It is also patterned after the church at Jerusalem. We read in Acts 2:5, 'There were dwelling at Jerusalem Jews, devout men, out of every nation under heaven'. Similarly at Syracuse University we have students and scholars from every nation under the sun as well as students from every State of the United States. This gives us both opportunity and responsibility to befriend and communicate the gospel. As they come to know the Lord Jesus Christ they are brought into the International Assembly where they can be discipled and became mature in the Lord. When they go back to their countries they are able to plant similar churches within their own cultural, national and linguistic backgrounds without compromising the revealed word of God.

PRACTICES OR THE ACTIVITIES OF THE CHURCH

The International Assembly has tried to emulate the New Testament principles practised by the churches at Jerusalem and Antioch. In Acts we read, 'And they continued steadfastly in the apostles' doctrine and fellowship, and in breaking of bread, and in prayers' (Acts 2:42).

Worship and the Lord's Table

Every Sunday morning believers would gather together for a time of corporate worship. All the believers, both children and adults, male and female, are encouraged to offer up their individual worship audibly one by one as the time allows. Worship is followed by the Lord's table, prayer, the ministry of the word of God and fellowship over a love feast.

Many visitors to the Assembly, both believers and non-believers, are challenged and encouraged by observing the worship service and fellowship. Let me give you a couple of examples.

Many years ago a visiting professor who was doing his PhD at Cornell University came to visit us. When he and his friend came the worship service was in progress in our living room. These two Hindu gentlemen sat quietly at the back and observed intently what was going on in the service. Believers one by one were pouring out their hearts before the Lord in worship and in adoration, some with tears. Jane, a newly converted student from Taiwan, was worshipping the Lord with tears streaming down her cheeks. After the service was over Mr Sharma said to Jane, 'You were praying as though you knew the person to whom you were praying.' Jane replied, 'Yes. I was thanking the Lord Jesus Christ who has become my Saviour and my personal friend since the day I accepted him a few weeks ago. According to the Bible, he is in our midst.' Mr Sharma was so impressed by her answer and asked her, 'But don't you go to church to worship God?' To that she replied, 'This is the church.' The Hindu man said, 'This is a house . . . and where is the steeple?' Jane could not answer him further and she brought him to me. He said to me, 'Sir, I was born and raised a Hindu. While I was in the university, I visited temples, mosques and churches looking for a God but I could not find one. So I became an agnostic. But today I sense a real peace in this place. I must say, if there is a God he is in this place.' When he said that, 1 Corinthians 14:25 came to my mind: 'And thus are the secrets of his heart made manifest . . . and report that God is in you of a truth.' I gave him a copy of the New Testament to read and he opened his heart to know more about the Lord Jesus Christ based on his experience at the worship service. Over the years many foreign students came to know the Lord by sensing the presence of God at the worship service and the love feast that followed.

Preecha and Anchalee Jengjalern were Buddhist converts from Thailand. While they were studying at Syracuse University we befriended them and discipled them. They were part of the Assembly for 6 years while working for their PhDs. One day, at the time of open worship where every believer is given an opportunity to worship the Lord audibly, they were surprised. They thought only pastors or church leaders were permitted to pray in the church while lay-people remained as spectators. Through worship and various other activities of the Assembly they came to know that the New Testament Church is an organism where every individual believer is equally precious, equally important, and equally necessary for the enrichment and the enhancement of the body of Christ. Now they are back in Chiang Mai, Thailand where they both are in a faculty of the University. They are living witnesses for the Lord Jesus Christ and are trying to apply the New Testament principles within the cultural background of the people of Thailand.

Friendship Evangelism: (Christ's Love in Action)

While the primary function of the Assembly has been worship or ministering to the Lord, the primary task of the Assembly has been evangelism among internationals at Syracuse University. Outreach to the university's 1;500 plus international students and scholars is based on the New Testament formula of 'a loving, caring and serving' church functioning as instruments of Christ's life, love, light, and liberty'. The ministry revolves around hospitality in the form of 'friendship meals' and other practical help to meet the needs of the people whom we serve in love. When new international students first come to the university we invite them to a friendship dinner where these 'strangers in transition' are welcomed, loved and befriended. While the university is in session we have weekly meals for them. Between 150–200 people come to enjoy the home-cooked meal where everyone is invited as our guests. For many years these meals were served in various homes, particularly at the Koshy home. Over the years, as the ministry has out-grown all the home facilities, large weekly meals are now served on campus facilities. Inviting foreign students, families and their friends to share food and fellowship in an informal, friendly, non-threatening atmosphere is the corner stone of the ministry.

We also provide practical assistance and counselling to international students who usually experience various 'shocks' after arriving in this country. The sudden changes include cultural shock, identity shock, linguistic shock, food shock, weather or snow shock, and above all, loneliness coupled with homesickness. Even though we try to serve them without any 'strings attached', yet initially many are suspicious of our motive. But as they discover the genuine Christ-like love which is the hallmark of this ministry, the 'walls' of suspicions and misunderstanding are broken down and the 'bridges' of understanding and friendship are made. Over the years many non-Christian intellectuals from various parts of the world have been won to the Lord and have gone back to their countries as living witnesses for the Lord. Let me cite a couple of examples.

Dr William Modugu was born of Muslim parents in

Nigeria. He with his family came to Syracuse to do his PhD. On a stormy winter night one of the members of the International Assembly met him and eventually befriended him and his family. First he was very sceptical of the love and friendship he saw in the International Assembly. He thought that was only a show but he kept on coming until he was conquered by the Christ-like love. He accepted Jesus Christ as his Saviour and Lord. Eventually his wife and children also came to know the Lord. After completing his PhD he went back to Nigeria. They got involved with a local church. Dr Modugu came back to Syracuse and I had the joy of baptizing him. Now he and his family are effective witnesses for the Lord Jesus Christ in Nigeria.

Ronald Rakiman and his family are another example. Rakiman is a gold medallist from Indonesia who came to Syracuse to do his Masters. He was touched and moved by the welcome dinner which was hosted by the International Assembly for new internationals. He wanted to know why we love people so much and serve them so sacrificially. When he knew we were constrained by the love of Christ, he said, 'I am a Muslim by faith but I am interested in knowing more about Jesus and the Bible. Will you please give me a copy of the Bible.' He enrolled himself in our weekly Bible studies for international students. He faced many problems in his studies. We prayed for him. We encouraged him to pray to the Lord Jesus. He experienced many answered prayers. That encouraged him to know that the Lord Jesus Christ is not only a prayer-hearing but a prayer-answering God. He prayed to receive the Lord Jesus as his Saviour and Lord. He committed his life to him. A few months later his wife arrived. Eventually she also prayed to receive the Lord Jesus Christ. Both were baptized before they went back to Djakarta, Indonesia. They are now actively involved with a local church.

During my visit to Djakarta in 1990 he introduced me to various local pastors. One pastor said to me, 'It is difficult to reach people like Rakiman who are educated and well-to-do Muslims in Djakarta but thank God, God used you to reach him for Christ while he was in Syracuse and sent him back to Indonesia to help us.' In this respect we are working as partners together in the work of the Lord globally. Many who came to know the Lord through the ministry of International Assembly are now witnesses for the Lord in various parts of the United States, Canada, Latin America, Europe, Australia, Japan, Korea, India, Pakistan and in several other parts of the world.

Our prayer is that the International Assembly may continue to function under the headship, lordship and kingship of the Lord Jesus Christ by the enabling power of the Holy Spirit in the light of the word of God. Through its functions and activities we may reflect and radiate the Lord Jesus Christ. Through the International Assembly the fullness of Christ, the unity of the body of Christ, the wisdom of Christ and the glory of Christ may be experienced, enjoyed and expressed. We are praying that the Lord may lead us to win at least 1,000 internationals for Christ by AD 2000. Pray for us that we may remain committed to the vision and the mission of the Lord till he comes.

Let us pray that Christians and local churches in every land may obey the command of the Lord in Leviticus 19:33,34.

'When an alien resides with you in your land, you must not oppress him. He is to be treated as a native born among you. Love him as yourself.'

'If you love me, keep my commandments.' (Jn. 14:15).

Epilogue

ROGER FORSTER

Many examples of churches being planted have been presented in the preceding pages. Only Latin America and Europe have been neglected in our survey. We apologise for this. Time and space have hindered our being more comprehensive in our review. However the phenomenal growth of the Evangelical Church in South America is well known to most if not to all. Again, in Western Europe, let alone Eastern, church planting is very much in evidence despite the historic parish church establishment which has been dominant in Europe for centuries. In the United Kingdom every major denomination including the Church of England, the State church, has church planting on its agenda and most of this agenda advance has happened in the past 3 years. The new churches in the United Kingdom grew by 144% in the 5 years up to 1989 and this was primarily accomplished by multiplying the number of congregations.

A few years ago the fastest growing denomination in the USA made an interesting discovery when comparing their figures with the fastest declining denomination. It was this: the churches in the fastest growing denomination who had not planted another church in the previous 5 years were compared statistically with those who had, and their newly planted offshoots. The non-planters were seen to be declining at the same rate as the fastest declining denomination but the planters and their offspring were growing so powerfully that they compensated for their fellow members' decline, so much so that the denomination taken altogether was in the first place of all denominations in their expansion. The statistics speak for themselves. Churches must plant, plan to plant, pray to plant and prepare for planting if we are to evangelize the world in depth. Christian mission is not completed by thousands or even by tens of thousands of decisions; it is completed by incarnations of the Lord Jesus being seen in every place, namely local churches.

In Matthew 13:47–51 Jesus gave us a parable of the kingdom. It is the parable of the dragnet. The kingdom is like a dragnet, every kind of fish is caught, in fact we must assume all the fish are caught since the sorting out of the good and the bad appears to be dealing with the whole of the human race and perhaps spirit powers too. It does not say there are any humans who could escape the judgement, so there are no fish who have swum around the net or got through a hole and are outside the net and are watching from a distance. All are gathered before him into the judgement of Matthew 25:31-33. The pulling in of the net is the end of the age. This is the time when Jesus comes again. Until now the kingdom has trawled the whole of the earth and has enmeshed the good and the bad alike till the great day of sorting out takes place, when everything evil is removed from the kingdom. Of course the kingdom is not the church. It is the release, the flow and the exertion of the Holy Spirit from the church. 'For the kingdom of God is not eating and drinking, but righteousness, peace and joy in the Holy Spirit' (Rom. 14:7). Or, seen in another way, Jesus defines the kingdom as the Holy Spirit's invasion from his body on to the earth and the situations in the earth. 'If I cast out demons by the Spirit of God, then the kingdom of God has come upon you (Mt. 12:28).' So now the kingdom flows from his body, the church, to effect God's will on earth in the same

way as it is done in heaven (Mt. 6:10). The kingdom of
God affects the immediate area surrounding the body of
the church and brings the good and the bad into its mesh,
guarding, keeping, but also restraining and overruling. At
Pentecost (Acts 2) the kingdom reached out and trawled
in 3000 fish – good fish; at the beginning of the Pauline
mission the Spirit fell on and trawled Ananias and Sapphira
(Acts 5) and Elymas (Acts 13:10-11) – there clearly are
bad fish. Kingdom netting must cover all the earth and
every fish then will be caught and then the end will come
(Mt. 24:14). It is therefore necessary to have 'power
points' i.e. local churches in every locality where human
beings, and even maybe spiritual forces, exist so that
everything may be ready for the moment of his return.

It would be possible, and I hope not irreverent, to
extend our Lord's parable of the kingdom (Mt. 13:51), by
introducing the church which is the instrument of the
kingdom. Just as I exert my rule or reign into the
immediate area around my body, my body-space I might
call it, so each local church extends its power, authority
and influence over its immediate neighbourhood by the
Holy Spirit. This is its territory or parish so that, using the
parable of the dragnet, we could say each knot of the net
is a local church and the four strands of rope reaching out
from that knot to the next knots are the kingdom, that is
the Holy Spirit acting into the area. Therefore when the
net is complete – no holes, no areas uninfluenced and
every knot is tied up to the next then the fisherman – our
Lord will pull in the net.

We need, or rather the Lord needs, churches powerful
in the Spirit in every area, reaching to the next church in
its area to thereby fill the earth with the Spirit of Grace
and Glory as the waters cover the sea (cf. Habakkuk
2:14: 'For the earth will be filled with the knowledge of
the glory of the Lord as the waters cover the sea.'). It was
said in one revival that you could feel the love of God a
quarter of a mile around the building where the church
was meeting. In another outpouring it was known in the
town by the very atmosphere that God had visited his

church, and in yet another place when God moved, the fishermen were drawn into their home-town, meeting on the quayside at 3 a.m. before their usual time of return and an atheist joined them who was so moved in his spirit that he had to come a considerable distance to meet with them on the quayside when God was there.

The net needs knots all over the inhabited earth. In a Western nation where there is great mobility and easy transport it was reckoned that over 50% of the church members lived outside the neighbourhood where their church building was situated. This is hardly taking ground for God; as pastors we must make room for three things.

1. The Holy Spirit (the net of the parable of the kingdom).
2. Reaching out to cooperate with neighbouring congregations (these are the knots of the nets).
3. Encouraging body life in the areas where our members live and in every neighbourhood where cell groups may exist. This will reveal Jesus, to back up our works of evangelization into all our neighbourhood.

When this is taking place in every nation and there is a church for every nation, when the gospel by the Spirit is going out towards every creature, then the net will be complete and Jesus will not be long coming. 'The Lord is not slow in keeping his promise, as some suppose, but is patient toward you, not wishing for any to perish but for all to come to repentance' (2 Pet. 3:9). He is in a hurry, he wants to come and he will come at that moment when the net has gone out into all the world.

We pastors are a great force. There are more of us than apostles and prophets, more of us than evangelists and teachers. We pastors are the key to reproducing knots of the right calibre all over the earth through our churches producing more knots and through those knots tying up in cooperation by the Holy Spirit to see the Good News going to all the world. May God help us in our great calling to see Jesus' heart satisfied and the church at last accomplish its purpose.

Contributors' Addresses

Ichthus Christian Fellowship (Roger Forster), 107 Stanstead Road, Forest Hill, London SE23 1HH, UK.

REACH International (John Richard), 3300 W. Mockingbird Lane, Suite 700, Dallas, Texas 75235–5992, USA.

Emmanuel Methodist Church (Rev. Dr. Martin P. Alphonse, Pastor), 48–50 Jeremiah Road, Vepery, Madras 600007, India.

Evangelical Church of India (Bishop Dr. M. Ezra Sargunam), No. 1, Second Street, Ormes Road, Kilpauk, Madras 600010, India.

OMF International (Tony Lambert, Director for Research, Chinese Ministries Dept.), Belmont, The Vine, Sevenoaks, Kent TN13 3TZ, UK.

Calvary Churches (Dr. Tissa Weerasingha), 123 High Level Road, Kirillapone, Colombo – 6, Sri Lanka.

Gereja Kristus Rahmani Indonesia (Dr. S.J. Sutjiono), Jalan Mangga Besar XI No. 34, Jakarta 11170, Indonesia.

Truth Lutheran Church (Rev. Peter N.Y. Yang), No. 86, Section 3 Hsin-Sheng S. Road, Taipei, Taiwan.

Kojo Church (Pastor Nabuo Tanaka), Chuo 2–1–15, Yonezawa-shi, Yamagata-ken 992, Japan.

Faith Community Baptist Church (Rev. Lawrence Khong), 66/68 East Coast Road, #06–00 Grth. Building, Singapore 1542.

Blackburn Baptist Church (Pastor Stuart Robinson), 27 Holland Road, Blackburn South, Victoria 3130, Australia.

Wesley Mission (Rev. Dr. Gordon Moyes), 220 Pitt Street, Sydney South, NSW, Australia 2000.

Faith Revival Church (Rev. Leslie James), P.O. Box 60790, Phoenix 6078, South Africa.

Dutch Reformed Church (Rondebosch) (Dr. Ernst J. van der Walt), Argylewed 9, Nuweland 7700, South Africa.

The Holy Ghost Revival Centre (Rev. Simon B. Azore), P.O. Box 7644, Accra North, Ghana.

St James Church (Rev. A.S. Thomas), Church of England in South Africa, P.O. Box 2180, Clareinch, Cape, South Africa.

Toronto Chinese Community Church (Dr. John Kao), 2230 Birchmont Road, Scarborough, M1T 2M2, Ontario, Canada.

Bethel Bible Fellowship (Dr. Willie O. Petersen), 17311 Dallas Parkway, Suite 238, Dallas, Texas 75248, USA.

Rolling Hills Covenant Church (Pastor James C. Creasman), 2222 Palos Verdes Drive North, Rolling Hills Estates, CA 90274–4220, USA.

Elmbrook Church (Dr. D. Stuart Briscoe), 777 South Barker Road, Waukesha, WI 53186, USA.

International Assembly (Dr. T.E. Koshy), 860 Ostrom Avenue, Syracuse, NY 13210, USA.